Practical Positive Potty Training

The Only Guide First-Time Parents Need to Potty Train Toddlers in 3 Days or Less

HANNAH BROOKS

Practical Positive Potty Training

Copyright © 2020 by Hannah Brooks- All rights reserved

No part of this publication may be reproduced, stored in a retrieval system or transmitted in any form or by any means, electronic, mechanical, photocopying, recording, scanning or otherwise, except as permitted under Sections 107 or 108 of the 1976 United States Copyright Act, without the prior written permission of the Publisher.

Limit of Liability/Disclaimer of Warranty: The Publisher and the author make no representations or warranties with respect to the accuracy or completeness of the contents of this work and specifically disclaim all warranties, including without limitation warranties of fitness for a particular purpose. No warranty may be created or extended by sales or promotional materials. The advice and strategies contained herein may not be suitable for every situation. This work is sold with the understanding that the Publisher is not engaged in rendering medical, legal, or other professional advice or services. If professional assistance is required, the services of a competent professional person should be sought. Neither the Publisher nor the author shall be liable for damages arising herefrom. The fact that an individual, organization or website is referred to in this work as a citation and/or potential source of further information does not mean that the author or the Publisher endorses the information the individual, organization or website may provide or recommendations they/it may make. Further, readers should be aware that Internet websites listed in this work may have changed or disappeared between when this work was written and when it is read.

FREE BONUS – 40 SCREEN FREE ACTIVITIES

Practical Positive Potty Training

It can be tough keeping your kids occupied indoors and not relying on TV. This is why I've prepared a Free book of the 40 Best Screen Free Activities Your children will love. Activities include doughs, goos, imaginative play in dragon and insect worlds, finger painting, bubbles and much more.

You can get all the necessary ingredients easily at the supermarket. Hours of fun, growth and development await!

Use the link below or scan the QR code to get your Free download instantly!

https://bit.ly/327uEgY

Practical Positive Potty Training

CONTENTS

Introduction **9**

What Is Potty Training, Exactly? **15**

    History of Potty Training 17
    It's Not Just Peeing In The Toilet 21
    A World of Methodologies 25
    Potty Training Infants: Myth Or Fact? 29

When To Start Potty Training **33**

    How Do I know if My Child Is Ready? 35

How To Start Potty Training **43**

    The Preparation 45
    Step By Step 49
    The Three-Day Method 61
    Why A Potty Routine is Important 67
    What You Need to Potty Train 69

How To Deal With Accidents (…And Success!) **77**

    What To Do When There's An Accident 79
    What to Do With Potty Success 83

Potty Training With Rewards **85**

    The Gold Standard: The Sticker Chart 87
    Gamify It! 89
    Other Forms of Rewards 91

Potty Training Pitfalls **95**

    The Second-Day Resistance 97
    Parental Pitfalls 99
    …And More 103
    It's Just Not Working 107

Potty Training In Other Cultures **111**

    How It's Done Across The World 113

Potty Training All Types of Children **121**

    Potty Training Girls 123
    Potty Training Boys 127
    Potty Training Children With Special Needs 131
    Potty Training Different Children 135

Potty Training: It's a Process **139**

    In the Still of the Night 141
    Continuing On the Road of Potty Training 145

Top 10 Tips for Potty Training, Straight From The Parents Who've Been There **149**

Conclusion **155**

INTRODUCTION

Potty training. It's one of those dreaded bumps in the road that every family must go through—but the reward is SO sweet: a fully functioning, portable, diaper-less child.

New parents always ask me this: is potty training really that difficult?

My answer is an emphatic NO. Potty training really can be simple and fun. There are a few key markers that can make or break your potty training experience, but the good news is they are listed in this book. You do NOT need to read a doctoral thesis, go to the doctor, or pay someone to help you potty train your child. You and your baby have what it takes to potty train, naturally.

My name is Hannah Brooks, and for years I have successfully helped parents potty train their children. While I do not physically put your little one on the toilet, I give moms and dads the confidence they need to start the training process and help them through any challenges they meet along the way.

As a behavioral and OT professional, I have met all types of families, each with their own difficulties. There is no issue I have not heard when it comes to potty training. I decided to write a book with all the tips and tricks that have brought success to my clients during toilet training.

I am also a parent of grown children, with babies of their own. I have personally used these techniques, and I have seen what works and what does not work, firsthand. Since every child is different, I am also aware that what works for one child may not work for another. Therefore, you will find different methods of training within these pages. If one training technique does not work, take a break and start over in a couple of weeks.

Before you know it, your toddler will be fully potty trained, and you will be free from diapers! Your child will have the confidence to tackle something new, and you will have the feeling of accomplishing a significant hurdle in your child's growth and development.

People thank me for giving them the support and tools to get through this time in their lives. However, at the end of the day, they need to be proud of themselves; I simply give them the toolbox and instruction manual. They put the pieces together, and you will too! The strategies in this book are the same ones I give to my clients. They are the same tools that have found success to so many families over the years.

Potty training your child does not have to be miserable. Yes, it takes some time and commitment, but in the end your child will eventually learn to use the toilet. Whether they do it now, in a stress-free way, or in a year or two, when you are feeling pressure to get them potty trained before they can go to elementary school, it will happen. So why not do it now, in a stress-free way, and avoid them having accidents in school, which can lead to embarrassment and self-esteem issues for your child.

Your child's brain is like a sponge, and their body develops the ability to control its urine and bowels as they grow. When you implement habits and routines that get them to use the toilet, instead of voiding in their diapers, it will become second nature to go to the bathroom to do their business. It is essential to help your child to navigate this time in their life and give them an incentive to use the potty like a big kid.

It is extremely important to be attuned to your child and to be wary of the window of opportunity. Each child has a window of time in which potty training will be much easier. It's essential to watch for this window and take advantage of it, so be sure to read this book around or before your child will be ready to potty train.

What Will I Get Out of This Book?

Whether you just found out you are pregnant or you have a toddler, one thing that may be weighing on your mind is getting down to business—potty business, that is. Potty training is something that all parents worry about, but rest assured, all children will eventually learn to use the toilet.

With my first child, a friend and parent once told me, "Don't worry. Your child will not still be wearing diapers to kindergarten." They were, of course, right. I worried for many months unnecessarily. To top it off, potty training was a breeze, so all that stress was for nothing. Sure, there were times that it seemed diapers were easier to use, like on long car rides. However, a few extra stops along the way were worth it, since my children were all totally potty trained in a matter of two weeks (pooping on the potty always takes a little more time than peeing on the potty. We will discuss that later in the book).

As if the freedom of movement weren't reward enough, potty training will save you money. When it comes down to it, diapers cost a fortune, and potty training your child will save you over $1,000 a year per child. That is money that can be used for other family expenses.

You also want your child to gradually gain independence. When they can successfully use the toilet without help from you, it is a huge milestone. As much as you love everything about your sweet little one, no one enjoys changing a diaper filled with poop. For that matter, no one enjoys poop exploding out of a diaper, either. You know the ones: when you have to pop your tot in the shower because they have poop all the way up their back and hardly anything in their diaper. How does that happen, anyway? These are the parts of having a baby that are, honestly, pretty gross. However, once they reach the toddler age, they are ready to lose the diapers and do the deed in the potty.

Not being potty trained in a timely manner can impact your child's ability to attend school. Many schools require a child to be totally potty trained before they can be registered. We will discuss this in greater detail in a future chapter.

Is Potty Training Really That Big a Deal?

Getting your child to use the toilet before they enter school is essential. Most educational institutions will not let your child attend pre-k or kindergarten before they are potty trained. Unless they have a medical condition that prohibits your child from using the toilet on their own successfully, they must be potty trained before entering school.

To prevent accidents during school, it is best to get your child potty trained before the age of four. Most parents begin potty training around the age of three; some even start at age two to two and a half. This allows their child ample time to get used to successfully using the potty before they attend school.

In This Book

In this book, we will discuss all aspects of potty training. I will give you the tools and resources to help potty train your little one with minimal stress. Whether you have a boy or girl, a child with special needs, have a child who is afraid to use the toilet, you'll find tips and tricks in this book. I will empower you to take the tools I share with you and use them in your home. Together we will get your child potty trained in no time, giving them the confidence to use the toilet. By the end of this book, you will have the resources to help your child to successfully reach their potty-training milestone, giving you both a little more freedom.

You will find tons of tips that you can apply in real time, even in the most tense or difficult situations with your child.

But above all, in this book, you will learn how to get through potty training in a relatively stress-free way.

Get Started

This book is guaranteed to help you overcome this big transition in your toddler's life.

The potty-training tips and tricks you will learn in this book are proven methods that yield positive results. Every chapter will give you information and actionable steps to help you navigate this time in you and your child's life. By the end of this book, you will feel confident that you are capable of potty training your child. If you stick to the routines and habits, you will have a successfully toilet-trained toddler in no time at all.

Don't wait to read this book. Potty training has an expiration date, and you do not want to miss your child's ideal window. Combining the knowledge contained in this book with the natural parental intuition and knowledge of your child, you'll take the effectiveness of your potty training to the next level. The potty-training tips that you are about to read have been proven to be effective. This book will give you a sense of hope and control over what can be a very messy process.

Practical Positive Potty Training

SECTION ONE

WHAT IS POTTY TRAINING, EXACTLY?

Potty training. If you're here, you probably know all too well what those two oft-dreaded words mean. However, for the sake of clarity and for anyone who isn't clear on what potty training is, let's look at what being potty trained really means.

Potty training, also known as toilet training and toilet learning, is the process of teaching a young child or infant to use the toilet for urination and defecation. Simple, right?

And if that is potty training, then when is a child officially "potty trained"? The definition of being fully potty trained is when a child independently recognizes their need to use the bathroom and asks to go to the bathroom accordingly. These definitions may seem simple, but the process is far more complex. What is in that training? What does it consist of? What parts are essential in the training? Which process will get us quickly from a child to a potty-trained child?

There is no one-size-fits-all easy answer. To get a better picture, let's step back in time and look at methods of potty training from the past.

Practical Positive Potty Training

~ 1 ~

HISTORY OF POTTY TRAINING

As long as humans have been around, they have been urinating and defecating. They have also been dealing with babies that don't know how to go on their own. So has potty training always been the same?

The answer to that question is a resounding NO.

Pre-1800s

Theories abounded in ancient times, and many of them involve children being left in their mess as they go about their day. However, it was also common to simply hold your child over a chamber pot or attempt to notice their signs and take them to the pot accordingly.

The 1800s

At this point in history, cloth diapers were the ubiquitous solution for children's bottoms. Secured by safety pins, when these cotton diapers were soiled, the caretaker would just hang them up to dry. If the child had a bowel movement, they would boil the cloth. However, awareness of bacteria grew, and parents began to attempt to potty train their children earlier.

Some Victorian texts encourage mothers to hold their children over the toilet at least twelve times a day.

1900-1950

Up until the 1930s, it was common for children to be put on laxatives so they would poop more regularly. This practice was quite widespread, along with the use of physical force.

At this time, the US recommendation for potty training age was 18 months, and it was called parent-led potty training.

Rumors began circulating that early, aggressive potty training could create a repressed rage, thanks to accusations leveled against Japanese soldiers by psychoanalysts.

1950-2000

Dr. Spock, a pediatrician and one of the best-selling medical experts in America's history, hit his stride right around 1950, and his "readiness" approach promoted a much more tolerant, child-oriented method of potty training. He urged parents to wait until their children were ready. This resulted in an increase of the age at which children potty trained across the board.

This encouragement to wait on potty training got some serious marketing dollars behind it in the 1970s, when the disposable baby diaper was introduced. Pampers invested in convincing parents to ease their strict potty-training schedules which, of course, resulted in a significant rise in diaper sales.

Sometimes, potty training was an expression of a culture. In East Germany, up to the 1980s, children were taught to use the bathroom with potty benches. Every child had to sit there until everyone was done using the bathroom.[i]

2000 and On

Technology has begun to creep into potty training in the form of apps and even the iPotty. This child's potty featured a dock for an iPad tablet, so that children could watch a screen while they poop. This creation was mostly panned by critics.

Practical Positive Potty Training

~ 2 ~

IT'S NOT JUST PEEING IN THE TOILET

Okay, we all know that the goal of potty training is for excrement to end up where it belongs—in the toilet. But the actual act of potty training is so much more than that.

A World of Skills

While potty training on your parental to-do list may take up just a single line, the truth is that there are dozens of mini milestones on the way to checking that box. Going to the bathroom, as simple as it now seems to us adults, is actually comprised of several interconnected skills. When you break them down, it quickly seems like a much larger undertaking than that single check would suggest.

Here is a list of these not-so-simple steps that make up a fully potty-trained child:

- Does not poop overnight
- Understands toilet training words
- Acts interested in the potty
- Can tell you if they've gone poop
- Poops regularly
- Stays dry for two hours or more

- Can sit on the toilet for at least five minutes without getting distracted
- Can flush the toilet
- Can tell you when they are peeing
- Understands how to pee in the potty
- Can wash hands alone
- Can pull underwear up and down alone
- Can pee in the potty with help
- Can tell you before they are going to poop
- Can use the regular toilet without a seat
- Can tell you they have to pee
- Wipes pee without help/Pees standing without help
- Has no accidents during the day
- Goes to the bathroom to pee totally alone
- Wakes up dry
- Goes to the bathroom to poop totally alone
- Wipes poop without helpii

Interestingly enough, the early end of these milestones usually occurs around two years. And the latter end of the spectrum occurs on the average at year three or even four. That means there's no rushing this long process. If you see it, however, as several mini accomplishments, you might just find that the process becomes more agreeable—and has more opportunities for celebration and positive reinforcement.

A Chance To Bond

As with any of life's most important milestones, potty training is not just about being able to go in the toilet. This is an opportunity to bond with your child, dressed up as a (slightly gross) chore. It's in these moments, when our children need our guidance and encouragement, that the bond of parenting is truly forged. Day-to-day life can easily become routine and slip past us. However, anything that takes us out of that invites us to wake up and pay attention.

Practical Positive Potty Training

Potty training forces us to snap out of autopilot. It forces us to tune into our children, their faces, their rhythms, and their needs. Use this chance and the built-in downtime it comes with to partake in activities that you both enjoy.

Practical Positive Potty Training

~ 3 ~

A WORLD OF METHODOLOGIES

There are as many ways to potty train as there are children. Finding out which one is right for your child is a matter of trial and error. Before you settle on your chosen method, it helps to have a broader overview of the most popular methodologies out there today.

Standard

For lack of a better word, there is the "standard" potty-training method. This method is a world unto its own, comprised of tips, tricks, rewards systems, and communication innovation. We will talk about more of these extensively in future chapters. Within this "standard" bracket lie two important distinctions: parent-led potty training and child-led potty training.[iii]

Parent-led potty training is what it sounds like—the parent chooses the when and instigates the steps of potty training according to their chosen schedule. Parents lead their child to the toilet according to a schedule of set time intervals, such as every two hours, or before and after naps and meals. Why choose such a rigid potty-training method? It is helpful when multiple caregivers are involved, as it is easy to follow and consists of outlined steps. It also means the family doesn't have to take drastic steps and block out the schedule just to potty train.

Child-led potty training is the inverse of this—the child initiates trips to the bathroom and sets the schedule. This relatively recent version of potty training was introduced in the 1960s, and it consists of reading a child's signs for readiness. It's backed by research and shown to be one of the more successful. This version is usually started when the child shows the desire to use the bathroom. The upside of this method is there is usually a lot less resistance and less tendency to slide backward.

3-Day

The three-day method is the most intense. It takes all the steps of potty training and combines them into three back-to-back, intense days. This method requires total attention and participation from parents, meaning you have to block off your schedule, cancel your plans, and get potty-ing. The good thing is if this method works for your child, potty training will be over and done with (the most important part, anyway) in just 72 hours.

The method consists of giving a big, ceremonious bye-bye to the diapers, then allowing the baby to wander and play in a safe space, naked from the bottom down. The idea is this helps them to get in touch with their urge to pee or poop and the feel of relieving those urges.

Elimination Communication

Elimination communication, or EC, is a type of toilet training that generally begins at a very young age, as early as one month! This practice consists of caregivers trying to tune in to their baby's needs in order to anticipate elimination, while working simultaneously to create a system of communication that allows them to know when their child is ready to urinate or defecate. The process revolves around the baby's bodily needs and rhythms. This type of toilet training is the norm in non-industrialized countries, where diapers are often a luxury that few can afford.

Elimination communication has four major pillars: timing, signals, cueing, and intuition. Timing is all about understanding your child's natural rhythms. The amount a newborn urinates is much more frequent than an older child. And you'll find that once you tune in, your child actually does urinate on a fairly regular schedule. Pooping is a different story, and is very personal. Some children may go several times a day, while others may go every other day.

Signals are the next pillar of elimination communication. Many children offer a subtle signal when they are about to eliminate, although these signals can be very different from one child to the next. Parents who do elimination communication keep their eyes out for signs like cries, squirms, and certain facial expressions. Discerning these signals often requires a diaper-free period.

Cueing is the part that many have heard about if they have heard anything about elimination communication. The cue is the sound or signal that comes from the caregiver and is meant for the baby. A particular noise is made to let the baby know when they should eliminate. This establishes an association that will help babies to go in unfamiliar settings that don't resemble their home potty. In many countries, this is a simple pssss sound.

Intuition is the X factor when it comes to elimination communication. This is the "tuned in" part, the one that will enhance the elimination communication training if there is a close relationship between caregiver and baby.

Practical Positive Potty Training

~ 4 ~

POTTY TRAINING INFANTS: MYTH OR FACT?

In the 1950s, Dr. Spock had some interesting theories on how to raise children, and one of these theories was that infants could be potty trained. Nearly 70 years later, there are parents who still subscribe to his methods and attempt to potty train their infant children.

Dr. Spock is not the only one who thought that potty training babies was a possibility. In other countries many children learn to use the toilet by 18 months old. We will explore this more later in this book.

The invention of disposable diapers is likely the main culprit when it comes to keeping children in diapers much longer. The magic of diapers is that the moisture created when a baby pees is wicked away from the skin, meaning baby doesn't feel wet.

Practical Positive Potty Training

In contrast, parents who use cloth diapers know that the diaper becomes quickly saturated when a baby urinates, and it creates an uncomfortable feeling against the skin. Babies who are raised with cloth diapers are said to potty train earlier than babies who wear disposable diapers. It is true that, in the 1950s when nearly all infants used cloth diapers, about 95% were potty trained by 18 months, whereas now the inverse is true. Only about 10% of babies are potty trained by 18 months.[iv]

Parents who utilize cloth diapers do so because they want to save money and because they feel a cloth diaper is safer for their infant than disposable diapers. These parents are also more likely to be the ones to attempt infant potty training.

So does infant potty training actually work, and how do you get a baby to use the potty?

As we mentioned in the previous chapter, this style of potty training is often called Elimination Communication, Elimination Training, or Natural Infant Hygiene. It is typically started between birth and four months old.

Advocates insist that toilet training their infants make for happier babies because they aren't wearing a wet, uncomfortable diaper. Many parents also find that their babies have less diaper rashes because the acid normally found in the baby's urine doesn't cause irritation to their skin.

Many studies[v] have been done to see if potty training an infant is a possibility. The real question to be asked is this: are you training your baby to use the toilet or have you been trained to bring your child to the bathroom when you sense that your baby is going to pee or poop? The true answer is the latter.

In order to properly toilet train your infant, wearing your undiapered baby in a sling or close to your body is recommended. In time you will learn the signals that indicate your baby will pee or poop, with the end goal of getting them to the bathroom before they make a mess all over you.

Practical Positive Potty Training

The amount of time and dedication this process takes is not for the weak; it certainly is not a viable option for many working parents, as daycares will not be on board with constantly bringing your infant to the bathroom. Only full-time parents are capable of properly executing this methodology. Why is that?

You need to be completely in tune with your baby and figure out what their voiding schedule is like on a daily basis. Does you baby pee within 20 minutes of having a bottle? Do they poop around the same times during the day? Does the schedule change when your baby has a growth spurt or starts eating solid foods? All of these situations need to be contemplated before deciding whether you want to attempt potty training your infant with EC.

When it comes down to it, most babies who were "potty trained" regress and are only fully potty trained by age two. Why is this?

A baby's body is not physically capable of recognizing the sensations of needing to empty their bladders nor are they able to control the muscles for controlling their bladder and bowel movements.

According to the American Academy of Pediatrics, the recommended time to start toilet training your toddler is between 18 and 24 months.

John Hopkins Medicine[vi] backs up these statements:

- A child younger than 12 months of age has no control over bladder or bowel movements.
- There is very little control between 12 to 18 months.
- Most children are unable to obtain bowel and bladder control until 24 to 30 months.
- The average age of toilet training is 27 months.

According to experts at the Mayo Clinic,[vii] some children are ready to start potty training between 18 and 24 months. However, most are not truly ready until around ages two and a half to three years old.

So how can an infant possibility be potty trained? In the end, potty training an infant is a form of conditioning. Due to the baby's level of development, this type of training is more about conditioning than full understanding. And, if the conditioning process doesn't go smoothly, there can be negative parent-child interactions and results, the most common being regression.

What exactly is potty-training regression, you may ask? Potty-training regression is when a child stops using the toilet and starts soiling themselves unexpectedly. These children go back to their initial habits and completely stop urinating or having bowel movements in the appropriate place.

While regressive behavior is common when potty training at any age, it tends to be more common among those who were potty trained as infants. This is due to the fact that the baby was not the one trained. Again, it was the parent who was trained to bring their baby to the bathroom at timed intervals.

There are some benefits to infant potty training. If you are able to get your baby to the bathroom on time, you will go through fewer diapers. As for being able to get your child fully potty trained as an infant, with no regressive behaviors or accidents, it is possible but difficult, especially in this day and age.

SECTION TWO

~

WHEN TO START POTTY TRAINING

While this isn't exactly a step in the potty-training action list, it is possibly the most important part of preparing to potty train. The moment you decide to begin potty training is a make-or-break moment. If your child is ready, it will go smooth and quickly. If your child is not ready, you are likely paving the way for power struggles, bumps in the road, and delays. Read on to see why, and how to choose the best time to begin.

Potty training is an important developmental milestone in your child's development. Just like talking, walking, and all those other less smelly ones, toilet training relies on the development of skills that, for the most part, need time to develop. It helps to think about potty training in this way, if nothing else than to take a bit of the pressure off yourself, and hence, your child.

Just like other developmental milestones, all babies hit them at different ages. There is no magic age that signals readiness to potty train. One child can show readiness and necessary skills at 18 months; another may show them at four years old. Gender can also have a say in this timeline—boys tend to run behind girls. If your child consistently hits milestones early, they may be a candidate for earlier potty training.

As with other developmental milestones, sometimes it takes a few days or weeks to truly get the hang of it. Yes, it's worth celebrating that first time in the potty, for sure. But it is far from the finish line.

~ 5 ~

HOW DO I KNOW IF MY CHILD IS READY?

One of the most asked questions I hear is, "How do I know if my child is ready to potty train?"

The answer to that question isn't always straightforward, but there are definite signs that parents can be on the lookout for that, when taken together, can mean a potty-ready baby. Some of these signs are physical; some of them are mental; and some of them are even emotional.

Physical Readiness

Signs of physical readiness are the most visible of all the signs that a child is ready to potty train. Here are some of them.

No poop overnight

This is one of the earliest signs of toilet-training readiness. When your child doesn't have a bowel movement during the night, it signifies they are gaining control of their bowels, an important part of toilet training.

Can remove clothing

It makes sense if your baby is to truly potty train, it is essential that they be able to remove their clothing. This is important for obvious reasons but also for the morale of your child. What you don't want is an accident that comes about because of a clothing malfunction.

Child is mobile

Having the ability to walk to the potty, whether you keep it in the bathroom or a room that your child spends most of their day, is an important part of potty training. If you child is not able to get to the potty on their own, it will be more challenging to potty train them when they start showing signs of preparedness.

Dry diaper after sleeping

This is actually one of the most advanced potty skills a child can have. If your child can nap or sleep through the night and wake with a dry diaper, they are definitely ready to potty train. This means that they are able to control their bladders are capable of maintaining that during the daytime.

When you start to notice that your child wakes up dry, it's a good idea to put them right on the potty. Your toddler may be able to pee in the potty or continue to hold it. But try to encourage urination. Turning on the water sometimes helps. You might also ask them to take a deep breath. This action tends to help your child to relax their bladder muscles just enough to start peeing. If they do pee in the potty, it is important to make a big deal out of it in a very positive way. This does not mean scaring them, but congratulating them with cheers, applause or, if you like, songs and dances.

Some parents find that sticker charts are helpful, while others reward their child with a favorite candy or food that is considered a treat. We will go over rewards in Chapter 3. The idea is to encourage peeing on the potty every time they need to go and when they do, your toddler will earn their reward.

Mental Readiness

Mental readiness is key as a measurement in readiness to toilet train. There are just some cognitive milestones that are necessary to reach before doing traditional toilet training.

Child can talk

Your child should be able to talk. Ideally, they will be able to speak enough to name the parts of the body and use toilet vocabulary. This increased level of communication is ideal for toilet training.

Parents who utilize baby sign language can show their child the sign for needing the potty and then show them what it means. This will mean walking them into the bathroom and showing them how you use the bathroom or having them sit on their potty seat. While it may take a little more time, especially if your child is hearing impaired and cannot hear the pee in the potty. However, your toddler is smart and they will catch on. In these scenarios, it is important to put your child on the potty when they have a full bladder, like after waking up in the morning or after a nap. Soon enough it will all become routine and normal to pee on the toilet.

Child knows they're wet

If your child is asking for a diaper change, or can tell you when they are wet or dirty, that is a great sign that they are ready to toilet train. Once they are able to feel the sogginess of a wet diaper enough to ask that you fix it, it's a good sign for toilet training readiness.

Child wants privacy to fill their diaper

If your child goes into a corner or in another room to have a bowel movement (or less commonly, to urinate), this is a definite sign they are mentally ready for toilet training. They know when it's coming, and what's more, they are ready to have their own space to do their business.

Emotional Readiness

This is a less obvious type of sign, but it's equally important for a child to exhibit emotional readiness for potty training. Potty training marks the beginning of a new way of life for your child, and that is a big deal. It can be scary, both for parents and for children.

Child exhibits confidence

Ideally, a child will exhibit security and confidence before starting the toilet training journey. They will be secure in knowing that their parents love them. Emphasize to the child how success in potty training has no link to the love they feel from you. Talk to them about all the other skills they have mastered, from eating, drinking, and putting on their clothes. These are all actions that once were too difficult for them, so potty training will be no different!

Child is interested

A child's desire to use the toilet is a big marker for potty training. Most children will start to express interest in the potty around 18 months. They tend to see others sitting on the toilet, since a closed door is not protection from a wandering toddler, and want to know why mommy and daddy go and sit on this mysterious seat every once in a while. If you have a little boy, and they see daddy standing up to urinate, this will be very entertaining to your toddler. Your son will probably want to try, too.

While he may not be physically ready to potty train, there is no reason that you shouldn't put out a potty seat and get him used to using the toilet. It is sometimes easier to potty train a boy when they are sitting down. Since children don't always have the capacity to coordinate urinating and aiming at the same time, having your son pull down his diaper and go through the motions of "peeing" is good practice.

The same goes for those with a daughter. If they express interest in using the toilet, too, encourage her to sit on the potty chair when you go to the bathroom. She can just sit there with her diaper on or pull it down and pretend to pee. Sometimes your toddler will surprise you and pee a little. This does not necessarily mean that they are ready for training, but it is an excellent opportunity to get excited about the fact they are getting closer.

Chances are, even if your son or daughter does pee a little in the potty, they will still follow you to the bathroom every time you get up to go. Most often, within a day or two, the excitement fades. Your child moves onto something new to do or play with instead of being fascinated with the potty. This is perfectly fine.

The practice of letting your child sit on a potty of their own shows them a few things. First, they get to see that it is not scary to sit on the toilet. Before a potty chair, their only interaction with the toilet may have been finding the handle and, perhaps, flushing a toy. If that happened, and they saw that once things fall in, they do not come back, it can be scary for your child. "What if I fall in?"

Second, your child will learn that peeing in the potty is absolutely normal and a part of life. Perhaps the fascination of using the toilet will wear off by tomorrow, but it is never too early for the potty seat introduction.

It's important to note that the absence of some of these characteristics doesn't mean that your child is unable to be potty trained; they most definitely are, pending a medical condition that prohibits their ability to hold their urine or bowels. But it may take a bit longer, or be up to the parent, or caregiver, to come up with other solutions.

When It's Not Just About Your Child

One factor to take into consideration when deciding when is the right time to start potty training is how close your child is to going to school. Many schools require a child to be totally potty trained before they can be registered. While some daycares of preschool programs will help you with potty training, there are some that will not. If you are considering sending your child to preschool, it is a good idea to ask about potty training and if help will be provided.

It's clear that there is a good reason behind the potty training requirement: teachers need to focus on educating the children in their class and cannot be responsible for helping them use the toilet all day. However, it can come as a shock to parents who haven't yet potty trained their children, or those who put their children in nursery at an early age. No parent wants their child to stick out, to be the one kid that's not potty trained, or to be embarrassed when they have accidents at school.

The exception to the "potty training rule" is if your child has a medical condition that prohibits them from using the toilet successfully on their own. Since schools are required to accept all students regardless of disabilities, or send them to an out-of-district school that would be better suited, a paraprofessional will typically be assigned to work with your child and assist them with their bathroom needs. On some occasions a nurse is needed to help your child. This may include changing diapers or assisting with hygiene practices. Good hygiene will be discussed about this later in the book. Since different states have different criteria and requirements for students who are unable to use the bathroom on their own, you will need to find out how this will be handled, should your child fall into this category of need.

Aside from being potty trained, so that the teacher can focus on educational material, a child needs to have the ability to go to the bathroom during the school day. If you child is not accustomed to using a toilet, and holds their bowels or urine, this can lead to serious medication conditions.

In severe instances, your child can end up with impacted bowels, and require medical intervention. Holding their bladder, and not urinating when necessary can cause urinary tract infections. No parent wants to see their child go through such painful (and preventable) problems.

When your child is physically ready, showing signs that they are capable of controlling their bowel muscles, it is the ideal time to teach them to use the toilet.

When You're Ahead (or Behind) The Pack

What if your child is significantly younger but is showing signs of readiness? Well…congrats! Some kids are just quicker at everything. Your toilet training experience may be different than your peers, for several reasons. Younger children won't be able to communicate as readily, to inform you of their needs. Nor will they be able to fully pull off their clothes, so that is a skill you should work on as quickly as possible. With a younger child, be very attentive in the first few days of potty training. If you see it's not clicking, just let it go.

Or maybe you're on the opposite side of things, and you've got a three-year-old who still hasn't shown interest or hasn't been able to successfully potty train. You need to start soon, because there will be hurdles that are unique to potty training an older child. Your child will likely be much more defiant, but you can counteract that with a casual, can-do attitude. The important thing is to be consistent. That is what your child is waiting on.

Whichever describes you and your child's situation, be ready ignore the haters and well-meaning advice givers, because there will be plenty. Follow your own intuition, informed by your amazing child and your relationship.

How Do I Know I'm Ready?

So, most of this book, and potty training in general, is definitely geared toward the child. Is the child ready? What does the child need to do? However, it is also important to consider the parent's readiness.

Everyone "wants" their child to be potty trained. But how much do you want it? It's good to assess your level of excitement…or is that desperation? It will help you to discern whether you are giving it a try or whether you are totally committed to potty training now. The giving it a try method usually ends up crumbling—it's better to see it as something that you are going to *do*.

Practical Positive Potty Training

Why are you going to begin potty training? It's important to examine your motivation for potty training. A good motivation is thinking your child is ready. A not-so-good motivation is your desire for your child to be the first in the class to be potty trained. Make sure the reasons you have for starting training are good ones.

It's also helpful at this point to determine your social media stance. I personally recommend keeping your child's potty training journey off of social media. It can be too defeating when it doesn't go as planned, or when there is a regression. Also, if your child gives you a hard time, it can be difficult to see comments from well-wishers urging you to do this or that, because "it will work so much better".

SECTION THREE

~

HOW TO START POTTY TRAINING

So, the moment has arrived. You think your child is ready to get rid of the diaper. You've studied their developmental progress and it looks right on track. They're in the optimum age range. They are even letting you know that they'd like to interact with the potty.

Faced with imminent toilet training, it may seem like a daunting process. In this section, I'll break down the how to, whether you decide to go with a child-led training or want to do it in three days. The first step is the most important, however: preparation! Don't skip it, as it can really smooth the path ahead.

Practical Positive Potty Training

~ 6 ~

THE PREPARATION

There is actually quite a bit you can do to grease the wheels before commencing potty training. To put it simply, what is easier? Going from lying on your back all day straight to learning to walk? Or first going through being on your tummy, then scooting, then crawling, and then, finally, walking? When phrased this way, it seems obvious that we should be taking small steps before jumping right in, doesn't it?

Here are a few great (and easy!) things you can do so that potty training doesn't come as such a surprise to your little one.

Talk About Using the Potty

You can start this one as early as your child's first birthday. Bring up the future potty training every now and then, in a fun and positive way, such as wondering aloud if your child's favorite cartoon character has to go to the potty. Talk about your need to go to the bathroom before you head to the toilet. Buy a book or two about potty training and keep it on the coffee table.

This has an informative aspect, too. Describe how your body tells you that it's time to go to the bathroom. Your little one will likely listen intently and even retain some of this. Drop the hint that, by going before you leave the house or before you start to play, you don't have to interrupt that activity to go to the bathroom. And don't forget to tell your child stories about your own toilet training experience—kids love knowing their parent was a child once, too.

Take Them to the Bathroom With You

Bring your little one into the bathroom with you, whether it's a number one or number two. They will be curious, innocently watching everything you do and in the process learning about potty training and learning about their body. Leave the door open while you go, and allow your child to take the initiative in checking things out. If your child has older siblings, they can help, too, just make sure that they are modeling good habits.

Introduce the Potty

Whatever potty you have chosen to commence the training with, keep it around the bathroom before beginning. Introduce your child to it before beginning, explaining to them this will be "their" potty. Them seeing it on a regular basis will be helpful for getting rid of any baseless fears before they form.

Let Your Child See Their Dirty Diapers

Occasionally, when you are changing your child, show them the dirty diaper that you are cleaning up. Tell them what you are going to do with it (clean their bottom, etc.). With a pee diaper, you can let them feel the weight of it to show where the pee goes. Don't make it out to be something disgusting; this is facts-only.

Get Your Child Excited

Potty training, if you think about it objectively, is pretty cool. *That* is the sentiment you need to pass on to your little one, anyway. Check out books on toilet training, find videos that are entertaining, and share them with your child. Focus on entertainment, but make it fun.

Don't forget to explain all the great things that come with using the potty—they'll be a big kid, they'll achieve a goal, they won't have to use diapers any more, and they will be in charge of their own bodies!

Prepare for Accidents

They're going to happen. The only question about accidents in the potty training process is where. Will it be on your precious Persian rug or on that white sofa? The best thing to do before potty training begins is to put away anything that could be damaged if pooped or peed on. That way, you won't have any triggers to have an explosion, which could be potentially scarring for your child.

Observe Your Child's Schedule

In advance of this day, be observant of your child's poop and pee schedule. It's often easier than you may think to trace a pattern around your child's bowel movements, and this information is gold when it comes to potty training. If your child is regular, and you put that schedule to work potty training, you are twice as likely to be successful, and fast! Don't worry if you can't discern a schedule, though. Not every child has one.

~ 7 ~

STEP BY STEP

Well, here we are! The big moment.

Whether you decide to begin potty training because you, the parent or caregiver, want to or because your child is showing interest and signs of readiness, the general process is what we will be covering over the next pages. First of all, congratulations on making the big decision. The most important thing is to keep a bit of perspective: every child ends up successfully potty training, so eventually this will end successfully! Stay cool and calm, expect a mess, and try to tune into your child's signs and signals to be able to help the process along smoothly.

In this chapter I will break down the different pieces of potty training in order, so that you can prepare yourself and your child for this big change. Each aspect of potty training (when, where, how, who, etc.) is broken down here in different sections, so read straight through or flip to a section that you have a special question about.

1. Pick A Day

This is a time of momentous change for your child. Yes, they already know how to poop and how to pee. But this day, they will learn a whole new place for doing so. For this reason, it's important to pick a day that will be stress-free, with no plans and nothing important on the agenda. Your child will need all your attention this first day, so be sure to pick a day in which you can be at home all day.

The night before the big day, explain to your child that tomorrow you will be with them all day, to help them start to use the big potty. Don't go too much into detail right before bed, though, or your child may not be able to fall asleep for excitement (or fear).

2. Be Normal

Anything that tips your child off that this is a huge, special day can actually feel a bit scary. Their suspicion sensors will be up if they sense that things are strange for some reason. Some parents I know make potty training a "go wild" day for their kids, offering sweets and junk food. However, in my opinion, this just gets the child riled up and feeling out of sorts, when what you really want on potty day is for them to be at ease and relaxed. Treat the day with a calm, positive attitude. Be matter-of-fact and slightly upbeat.

3. Start The Day!

On this first day, you'll want to wake up before your child if at all possible. Around their normal waking time, gently raise the blinds, sing a song, or do anything else that you think will wake them up on the right side of the bed. Take them directly to the bathroom—this is your child's diaper removing ceremony. If you can get your child to use the bathroom in the toilet for the first pee of the day (it's almost certain they need to go), then you are already headed in a positive direction. Whatever the outcome, find an aspect of the attempt to praise, and then it's time to begin the day.

If you notice that your child is waking up with a dry diaper a few days in a row, this is an excellent sign that they are starting to have control over their bladder functions. At this point, you can do two things, wait a little longer to see if it is a fluke, occasional wet diapers in the morning aside, or put them on the potty seat when they wake up in the morning. If you go for over a week or two with dry diapers every morning, it is definitely time to start putting them on their toilet in the morning.

By having them void in the toilet first thing in the morning, two things can happen. One, they will pee in the potty a lot and start to understand what it feels like to have to pee and what it feels like after they void.

Be sure to use phrases like:

"Yay, you are going pee-pee in the potty!" (big smiles)

"Don't you feel better now that you went pee in the potty?"

4. The Diaper Goodbye

The first activity of the day should always be the Diaper Goodbye. It's up to you and your child's individual level of theatrical drama or enjoyment as to how big a deal you make of it. You can simply remove their diaper and say "Today you are going to put your pee in the potty, like a big boy!" Also mention that you will help them do so, and that it's actually pretty fun! If your child has more of a flair for the dramatic, make a big song and dance about it. Take each diaper one by one, for example, and throw it in a garbage bag, saying in funny voices "We don't need you any more, diapers!"

Also a note, especially to parents that tend to do this on a regular basis anyway: today is not the day to ask "Are you ready?" You should avoid any opportunity for them to say no. We've already established that your child is ready. Tell them they're ready, and don't even finish your pep talk with an "Okay?" It may be hard but you can do it!

5. To Dress or Not To Dress

Now that the diapers are gone, and you may have scored your first victory with an early riser pee, it's time to get serious. Before you set out on your potty training day, you need to make a decision that plagues many a potty training parent: naked, underwear, or Pull-ups?

What to wear down there when potty training is important for your child. The fabric (or lack thereof) that you choose will influence how your child perceives their bowel movements and urine in the case that they don't make it to the toilet (and let's be honest, that's going to happen to 99.9% of you, at least once). Have you thought about which one you would like to use? Nothing is wrong with any option, however I have a definite favorite.

Nakedtime

Hello, nakedtime! In my experience with children, being naked from the waste down is, hands down, the best way to ensure a good start to toilet training. Every ounce of determination and awareness should be optimized for maximum success, and this first day is key. That's why I like to remove any barrier that might prevent one of those amazing early successes, which make your children feel so good: getting that pee or poo into the toilet.

Does this mean that your floor will likely be dirtied, multiple times? Yes. But it means that you will likely take strides instead of jerky baby steps, which is what you and your child need on that first day.

So how do you do nakedtime? Essentially, it's nothing more than having your child go bottomless and engaging fully with them near a bathroom or potty. Generally, children have a blast! And as a parent, it's a great time to give your child your undivided attention, which in today's world isn't as easy as it used to be. Here are a few tips to pull it off:

- Prepare by deciding where you will do nakedtime, and have anything you'll need to clean (paper towels, disinfecting spray, sponges, etc) nearby.

- If your child usually goes to the bathroom at a certain time, start around that time. If not, begin at a convenient time for you.
- Start by just letting your child go bottomless.
- Do not make nakedtime about potty training; don't even mention it until the first "accident" happens.
- Pay close attention to your child and their body language.
- When it comes time for a possible elimination, engage your child in conversation about what might happen.
- When something does happen (urine or a bowel movement),

Nakedtime allows children to see up close and personal what happens after you eat and drink. It allows them to get past the typical barriers and to connect them with their instinct. Once they make this connection, I find that then it makes more sense to bring underwear back. Think about it: allowing them to see the immediate effects of the bodily function they can feel is a powerful teaching tool. Once they see that, then they have the knowledge they need to later put into practice the idea of going to the potty when those feelings arise. It is only at that point that I advise adding the clothes back into the mix.

But isn't it…messy?

Now you understand the logic behind nakedtime. But maybe you're having trouble picturing the logistics. A naked child running like crazy around the house? What about all your carpet? Yes, nakedtime can be messy. And I definitely advise doing it in uncarpeted areas of your house if at all possible. I have found great success with parents who do nakedtime in the backyard, which can be fun for everyone, and means less cleanup for parents. Just be sure to use footwear that is either easy to spray off or can be tossed in the case of a messy accident.

The first elimination

No matter how good your child is or how easily they adapt to potty training, there will always be at least one "accident"—the first. That's because it's not really an accident; this is the chance for observation and teaching. Don't look at this accident as problematic. This is your teaching moment. Here's what to do:

- Comment matter-of-factly about what has happened. This is important because sometimes kids won't notice, especially if they have only just started peeing.
- Be sure to convey this is normal, and happens to everyone.
- Speak in calm, relaxed tones.
- Casually show them the potty, and explain they can use this next time so it's not so messy.
- Offer them the option to sit on the toilet.
- During cleanup, be very casual and do not make a big deal about the mess.

Pull-ups and underwear

In my experience, pull-ups can really serve as more of a setback or a crutch than a helpful potty training tool. To your child, it feels like a regular diaper, serving up little motivation for them to begin to use the potty. To you, it's much more of a hassle to change than a regular diaper, often resulting in messy smears all over your child's legs. I only recommend pull-ups as a special tool for exceptional moments, such as long car rides or travel.

Training underpants are a sort of middle ground between pull-ups and underwear. Again, I recommend these for later in the process, or for children who are very particular or headstrong about what they are wearing.

As I mentioned above, I also don't recommend moving straight to underwear, as that can result in fewer effective pees and poops in the potty, which can be defeating for a child. Best to use underwear a bit later in the process, when there is already a link to the need to pee with the potty and your child has developed a bit of bladder control.

I personally like to look at underwear as a before and after marker in the toilet training process. With underwear, I always say let the child choose. If they are expressing an intense desire and interest in wearing them, then you have just been granted a great bargaining chip. Let your child know that they can wear the new underwear as long as they give it their best go when you remind them to use the toilet.

If your child can control their bladder somewhat AND is showing interest in underwear, this is a great signal that daytime diapers should be gone forever. Just be sure you are ready to commit. Once you make this decision, the rule of thumb should be to transition in the morning after waking up to underwear and then not return to the diaper until it's time for bed.

6. Drink

Making sure your child is hydrated gives them the raw materials for success. Be sure to lead them to drink several times before and during your toilet training sessions. Give them an extra glass of water at mealtimes, and then whenever they ask or whenever they accept your offer for more. Do not, however, go overboard, as that can cause irritability and actually make it hard for your child to avoid accidents.

7. Props

Potty training isn't without its toolkit. For the big day, there are definitely a few items you shouldn't be without (like a potty!). However, you'll also find that a lot of what people bill as essential is actually superfluous. Skip to the next chapter for a full list of what to buy and what to skip.

8. Toilet Sitting Sessions

Okay! So baby is awake, has had some water or something else to drink, and is naked from the top down. Now what?

The procedure I've found as the most helpful when it comes to sitting sessions is to combine the child-led toilet trip with scheduled potty sitting sessions. These scheduled sessions are useful for children who aren't sure how to tell or are having too much fun to tell. Also, being flexible and allowing your child to dictate a trip helps them to gain mastery of knowing their own bodily signals. You should also be watching for signs, as you can help achieve that goal by seeing a need, naming it out loud, and taking them to the toilet.

However, all that doesn't mean that you should be asking your child every five minutes if they need to go to the bathroom. These toilet sitting sessions are meant to complement any self-prompted trips your child makes to the bathroom, and they should take the form of regularly scheduled programming, ie, every 30 minutes or so.

What to do if you tell your child it's time for a sitting session and they give you a flat-out NO?

Take a step back and try to figure out why. Is your child doing something they find interesting? Often, young children are so involved in what they are doing that they don't even process what they have heard for up to a minute. Be sure that your child has had time to hear, process, think, and respond. If they do so, and then you still meet with resistance, tell them clearly that after five more minutes have passed, it's time for a bathroom break.

Another reason your child may say no is they may be telling you that they do not actually have to go to the bathroom. In this case, you really want to avoid any kind of forced bathroom break. One of the cardinal rules of potty training is avoiding power struggles, because they create a negative atmosphere around what is really just another daily bodily function. We want to avoid this at all costs.

9. Watch for Signs

Yes, the end goal of potty training is a child who knows the signs and how to recognize the need to use the bathroom and takes action. But there is so much ground to cover between being diapered and using the potty. Think of your ability to watch for the outward signs that your child needs to go as those little blow-up floaties children wear when learning to swim. They can make the difference between success and failure, and what we crave in this process is most definitely every little success we can log.

Fortunately, when it comes to the potty, you can probably read your child like a book. There are some telltale signs that many children exhibit when they need to use the restroom. Here are some of the most common. Watch for them when you are potty training your child, and at the first glimpse of any of them, either offer the bathroom or encourage them to accompany you for a sitting session.

Getting antsy

This is probably the most common telltale sign. Many children start to wiggle and fidget if they have to go to the bathroom. It's even got a name: the potty dance. Be wary of this sign and be sure to invite your child to go to the bathroom if they start to show antsy, hyperactive behavior.

Hiding

This is more common when a child has to defecate. Many children hide when pooping, looking for that extra privacy. Whisk them off to the toilet if you find them hiding! But be sure to leave them on their own once they are settled on their potty, because, after all, what they need is a moment to themselves.

Squatting

This is another dead 'poop' giveaway. Squatting is a position that many children favor for passing a bowel movement. If this is one of your child's cues, then they will probably prefer a low-to-the-ground toilet.

Grabbing themselves

This is another one of the most common signs that a child needs to go to the bathroom, and it can persevere into late childhood. It helps them to hold in their pee, both mentally and physically. However, it is also a sign that tends to show late in the process, when your child really needs to go. Be firm if you see them exhibiting this sign, and get them to the bathroom as soon as possible.

Farting

Many people (not just kids!) find themselves passing gas as a prelude to executing a necessary bowel movement. Your child is likely no different. If you hear or smell your child farting, make it a teachable moment and let them know that this is connected to the poop that they can put right in the potty.

Crossing their legs

This is similar to the grabbing sign. This motion helps your child to hold in the pee or the poop while they go on about their merry way. It's hard to remember just how tough it is to tear oneself away from an amazing toy or playing with friends, but know that the struggle is real for small children. The last thing they want to do is to leave their toy unattended to go to the bathroom.

10. What Happens on the Pot

This combination of nakedtime and you being clued in to your child's sign is the foundation of a solid potty training.

What happens on the pot, however, will depend greatly on what kind of child yours is and the moment you have chosen to begin potty training.

Much to your chagrin, when you plop your child on the potty, you may get a big old NOTHING. Your toddler might want to try to hold their urine for as long as possible because they aren't used to the sensations yet. Even if they sit on the toilet, your toddler still might not relax their bladder muscles enough to urinate. This is okay. The fact that they can control those muscles to hold it in is a great start. Try not to pressure them if this happens. You do not want to force things or make your child feel like they did something wrong. The best thing to do is congratulate them for sitting on the potty and try getting them to use the potty in a couple of hours.

Perhaps, however, when you put your child on the pot, IT HAPPENS! Congratulations, first to you, and then of course to your child. Make a big deal. As big a deal as your child's threshold for excitement can handle. I have a whole chapter on rewards and positive reinforcement, so be sure to read it.

11. And, Repeat…

Potty training (normally) is not a one-and-done process. As the parent, your job is to translate each bit of progress as a major success to your child. It is a nourishing cycle; the more successful your child feels, the better a job potty training they will do. If your child is showing off each poop and pee in the potty to you, that means you have managed to make them feel motivated—great job. Always look for that opportunity to praise them.

I have written a whole chapter dedicated to how to deal with accidents, as well as successes, so if that's what you're wondering right now, then skip ahead to Chapter ~ 11 ~.

This process, from nakedtime to the incorporation of pants and underwear, can stretch on for a few weeks. It is of the utmost importance that you be aware of your child's signs and evaluate when they are ready to progress. As soon as you see signs of progress, it's time to apply just a bit more pressure to keep the potty training moving forward. It will be difficult, but don't stop! You've come so far already.

Practical Positive Potty Training

~ 8 ~

THE THREE-DAY METHOD

To put our own spin on a popular saying, there's more than one way to toilet train a child. There are many variations, and while I've referred to the option in the previous chapter as "standard," the truth is that many, many families opt for trying the three-day method.

The three-day method is, as it sounds, an intensive three-day all-holds barred potty-training session. If that doesn't sound like your cup of tea, well, rest assured you're not alone. However, the method has proven to work for some children, and what parent wouldn't want to have potty training more or less finished in just a long weekend? If the prize seems worth the sacrifice, then the three-day method might be for you.

In this chapter, I'm going to run through the steps of this method. I find that the standard method has more reliable results and is less frustrating for the parent, but I do feel that if the standard method is just not working for you, it's important to try something new, too. That's why I'm including the outline of this popular method, so if you like it, do a bit more research before trying it out.

The three-day method shares some aspects in common with the standard method. For example, it is vastly important to choose your timing carefully before starting, and perhaps even more so since the three-day method is such an intense jump into potty training.

1. Talk It Over

The bottom line is—communication is an essential part of a parent-child relationship, and when it comes to potty training, it's vital. In this case, it's vital because your child wasn't born with the language to express their potty needs. They will look to you to help them understand how to vocalize that urge. Talk as much as possible about going to the bathroom, so they can absorb the phraseology. Then, make an official introduction to the potty for your child. Even if it feels redundant, it's important to introduce your child and the potty officially.

2. Choose Your Three Days

Select three consecutive days that you will be able to dedicate yourself fully to potty training efforts. Commitment on your part is essential for the three-day method to work. One of the potential downsides to this method is you absolutely must be all eyes on your child. Consider locking your phone up for the weekend, because this method requires that level of commitment.

3. Diapers, Goodbye!

The first step in this method is, on the first day of the three, to say goodbye to diapers. Create a scavenger hunt or some other fun-filled method to find all your child's diapers. Together, you should both throw them "away," storing them in a box or trash bag, because this is the end. The goal of this step is to convince your child that they are gone for good.

4. Get Started

Let your child go bottomless (or totally naked) and set up shop in the room you have chosen, near the bathroom that your child will be using. Use a firm statement to remind your child often about using the bathroom. When I say often, those who use this method generally will repeat their phrase every five minutes or so. A good example would be, "Tell me when you have to go to the bathroom." Notice how this is a statement, not a question, and it doesn't invoke your child's wishes or desires.

5. Hydrate And Hydrate Again

Once you've gotten the day started, your next duty is to get your child to drink. Let them choose what they'd like if you're having a hard time getting them to drink a lot of water. Ideally, they will drink enough so that they are going to the bathroom many more times than usual. Each time they either succeed or fail at going to the bathroom, it's great practice for them. And the more practice you have in three days, the better.

6. Stay Together, All The Way To The Toilet

From now until the three days are up, you must remain glued to your child's side. This is important throughout the duration of the training, but it's so, so important at the very beginning. When your child has their first accident, which is almost certain, you need to be right there to attempt to move them quickly to the potty. If you are quick enough, you may get a bit of that pee into the potty, or your child may abruptly stop peeing when you scoop them up, which means they could likely still have some pee for the toilet.

7. The Treat

It's also helpful to take them to the potty about five minutes after the first accident and potty sit, as the big fuss around the first accident may have frightened them into holding some in. Have them sit for about a minute, and then reward them with a treat, one that you have a stockpile of and that will truly motivate your kid. These treats are for each time your child pees in the potty (except for this first treat, which is to illustrate what will happen). I find with this method it is very helpful to keep track on a notes app or a piece of paper when your child drinks and when they use the bathroom. Also keep in mind that you don't have to remind your child so often in the half hour after they go, as they will likely not have an accident right after going.

8. Praise Them

Any trip to the potty, whether fruitful or not, should be accompanied with an abundance of praise. If the trip was preceded by an accident, you'll want to address that accident, but do so from a teaching perspective rather than a chastising or punishing one. Remember, your child doesn't really know what they are supposed to do at first, so by wetting themselves, they haven't done anything wrong. Show them the difference between wet and dry underwear.

9. Repeat

That's it! Repeat these steps and that is the sum of the three-day potty method. While it is admittedly labor intensive, it also is a quick way to training your baby on the potty if you stick with it.

10. Okay, Actually It's 10 Days

The three-day method generally achieves a certain level of potty training before three days are up. However, to form a new habit, your child needs more time. Experts recommend sticking with the program for 10 full days, so be sure to set aside 10 days for the entire process before giving up. And, of course, potty training is a multilayered process, so after the first or second day, you can start to put pants on your child, take them outside of the designated potty area, and do other things that will help simulate the real world for your child.[viii]

Practical Positive Potty Training

~ 9 ~

WHY A POTTY ROUTINE IS IMPORTANT

Good routines are important to establish at the start of potty training. The more that using the potty is part of your child's regular day, the faster they will accept the toilet as the place to go to do their business. Consistency is key.

Routines are essential for children. They eat at a certain time of the day, take naps regularly, and go to bed at the same time most nights. Using the toilet should be just the same. If you get your child used to using the potty at the same time every day, they will quickly catch on to the practice. I recommend the following schedule as a jumping off point, while you find the natural rhythms of your child.

- first thing in the morning
- midmorning
- before lunch
- before nap
- after nap
- before dinner
- before bed

It's also helpful to make a habit of going to the bathroom before you leave the house. This is the essence of infant potty training theory: for parents to get their child on a toileting schedule.

The importance of routine for children is a well-established fact. However, having a potty routine also helps your child's many caregivers. Keep a record of your child's potty routine, and use it to communicate with caregivers, partners and daycare instructors. Ideally, the routine will include habitual potty break times, pee frequency, poop timings, and even your child's habitual potty songs. Give this plan to any caregivers in advance so they can ask questions and clarify any part necessary.

Even if you are working and only at home with your child during the mornings, evenings, and weekends, you can still have a routine in place. Children are marvelously adaptable, and they are able to compartmentalize the different figures and places in their life. Setting an agenda helps you to maintain this consistency and feels good for your child.

Above all, be sure to incorporate into your routine that same positive, relaxed attitude that I mentioned before. Making your mind up and committing to keep it positive is the best thing you can do for your child when they are potty training. It helps to reduce overwhelm and to encourage your child in this journey.

~ 10 ~

WHAT YOU NEED TO POTTY TRAIN

There's no doubt that potty training has become its own mini industry in America. Pull-Ups are the perfect example, a whole new category of underpants that didn't exist until a company figured out they could exploit the fears of confused parents. Anything that corporations think they can sell you related to potty training, they will. That explains the multitude of potties, clothes, toys and books related to potty training.

In this chapter, I'll review what is truly essential for the potty training process. I think you'll find it's a lot less stuff than you'd been led to believe. That doesn't mean to say that if you, as an adult, are excited or drawn toward a frivolous item you can't buy it for you or your child. However, I know many of you want to get the bare minimum that is necessary to get you through this phase. So in this chapter, I am breaking apart the essentials and the frivolous, to allow you to make an informed decision.

The Essentials

Even for the most minimalist potty training parent, there are some must haves. You can purchase most of these items without breaking the bank, and they are definitely essential investments:

The Potty

The most obvious, most important piece of toilet training tops our list: the potty.

The first question a parent must pose is the choice between a potty chairs, a potty insert, and nothing, or using the regular toilet. Unfortunately, there is no straightforward answer. The "right" answer will be one that takes into account what you the parent wants, as well as the personality of your child. It doesn't end there, however—your child will give immediate feedback, and it's up to you to potentially adjust if the potty training doesn't go well.

Let's look at the pros and cons of each option, starting with my preferred option:

The Potty Insert

Potty inserts, also known as potty seats, are round seats similar in appearance to a toilet seat. They are smaller, however, and designed to sit on top of a toilet seat. They reduce the size of the toilet hole, so that your child doesn't fall into the toilet. The genius thing about this option is that the poo and pee go straight where they belong—into the toilet. This is obviously great for adults, as it means no more cleanup is necessary, but it's good motivation for "big" kids, too.

Pros:

- So much less cleanup
- They are much closer to the real thing
- They make the transition to big potty, as well as peeing while out of the house, much easier

Cons:

- They may not work for children younger than two years, as the larger toilet may be just too intimidating.
- They require a step stool for most children to be able to reach
- They normally must be removed for an adult to use the bathroom
- Children generally need supervision during use

The Potty Chair

A potty chair is a tiny little seat that resembles an old-school toilet. It has a seat with a hole under it, which is typically a removable insert. When the child does their business in the potty chair, cleanup is usually done by removing the basin insert and dumping it into the real toilet to flush before cleaning it out. This standby of potty training parents often gets great results, but it has a few real downsides.

Pros:

- They're cute and kids love them
- They are portable, meaning they can be set up anywhere
- They're easy to access for kids, and can reduce accidents for kids in a hurry
- They allow children to use without any help, promoting independence

Cons:

- Requires parent cleanup to get rid of poo and the dreaded number two
- This is the furthest option from a real toilet, so the transition may be difficult
- It takes up space in small bathrooms
- It can look too much like a toy, and some children may end up playing with it

The Toilet

There are those who potty train right on the toilet. This is a more popular option with parents whose child is on the older end of the scale. It's a great option for kids about to start daycare, since in daycares children almost always use the toilet

Pros:

- So much less cleanup
- Avoids purchasing more "stuff"
- Teaches children the real way of using the bathroom from the beginning

Cons:

- It may be frightening for some children
- Most children need a step stool either to reach the toilet or to prop their legs up for pooping
- It can cause an increase in accidents due to being more difficult to access
- Children need supervision during use

Underpants

Underwear is one of your greatest tools in potty training. First, for obvious reasons: the change from diapers to underwear is a drastic one. It is a fabulous way to mark pre- and post-potty training. It will seriously stand out in your child's mind—the day they became a "big kid"—so be sure to use it to your advantage.

Another great thing about underwear is that it really gets kids excited about potty training. It's amazing how motivating a simple pair of undies with a favorite character or color on them can be. By all means allow your child to take part in the selection of the underwear, as this will only increase their effectiveness. Take your child to the store, let them pick out their favorite pair.

Underwear have another upside, as well. The reason why I recommend it over pull-ups or training pants is that it allows your child to really feel wetness. They will know the second they have wet themselves, whereas with diapers and pull-ups the wetness is wicked away and disguised, making them not much more than glorified diapers.

The Useful

These items are items that I would say are almost mandatory but not quite. They are extremely helpful in your potty training journey, and I highly recommend them to facilitate the entire training process.

Step stool

This is important if you are potty training a child younger than four, which is likely the majority of potty training cases. A step stool serves two purposes: one, to help a child get up to their toilet seat or the big toilet. Secondly, the step stool is useful when your child is trying to go number two on the toilet. It's a proven fact that in the West, we have adopted a posture that doesn't help loosen our bowls at all, and in fact the higher up your bent knees are, the better you go. And don't we want to facilitate as much as possible for our little poopers?

Even if you are starting potty training with a potty chair, a step stool always comes in handy for kids, and eventually they'll need it to be able to experiment with the big potty, so I recommend just going ahead and getting one.

Elastic-waist pants

Much of potty training is about removing obstacles. The elastic-waist pants may seem like an afterthought, but achieving those early successes is so important that it's a shame to let a few buttons and zippers get in the way. I definitely recommend having several pairs of leggings or other elastic-waist pants on hand during the process, as they will be much easier for your child to pull up and down themselves.

Plastic mat

A plastic mat or sheet is a useful thing to have if you have a sofa or other chair that you need to protect from accidents. It will give you some much-needed peace of mind when your little one is perched on a new sofa while potty training.

The Fun

Potty training can also be fun (yes, really)! It's a stressful time for some, but it's all about how you approach it. As a parent, there are interesting ways to gamify potty training, which we will get into in more detail later in the book. For a child, having these fun extras around can make the difference between misery and memories.

Watch

There are many inventions around the world of potty training, some of them more suspicious than others. One that was initially skeptical of at first is the potty watch. This contraption is a watch that counts down to the next potty time, and when the time is up, it flashes, makes fun sounds and songs, and in general grabs a child's attention. For some kids, I have seen it work wonders.

Stickers

Stickers are a great rewards system, and there are many ways to employ them. I'll speak more about specific ways later in the book, but one fun option is to allow your child to decorate their potty chair or toilet seat with stickers of their choice.

Treats

By treats, I am referring to anything that your child loves: candy, books, small toys, anything! Choose what you will use as a potty motivator, and be sure it's on hand before you begin training.

The Frivolous

The flip side of knowing what to buy is knowing what to not waste your money on. That's why I think it's important to list the following items, which I consider to be a waste of money. If you have bought or really want to buy these things, don't feel bad. However, for those looking to streamline or for those with an easygoing child, I just don't think they are necessary.

Costly or strange potty chairs

There is a world of potties out there for kids beginning to potty train. And as I mentioned, there are loads of companies just trying to squeeze every dime they can out of you, the parent. Some of these potties are large, designed to look like a real potty but more accessible so that children can feel comfortable on them. Other potties are themed, play music, or do other things to try to catch your child's attention. I believe that the focus should be on using the bathroom when on the potty, and any outside coercion can happen in the form of a well-thought out rewards system, so I say pass on these.

Portable potty chairs

These are fold-out toilets that you carry around with you. The basin of the potty is a pad, similar to a diaper, and you just throw it away when your child is done doing their business. This is another one I don't see as being worth it. Take a diaper for those times when you can't get your child to a clean-ish toilet.

Portable toilet inserts

These are the same as the above—I just think they are too much trouble to bother with. Imagine toting this around to a crowded football game or holiday picnic. It's much better to use wipes and hand gel for cleanliness.

Practical Positive Potty Training

SECTION FOUR

~

HOW TO DEAL WITH ACCIDENTS (…AND SUCCESS!)

In all of the preparatory excitement when it comes to potty training, I find that parents often forget to think through what they will do and how they will react when it all goes down. It is so important for parents to get in the zone in this regard. You want to have thought through your desired reaction in the case of an accident before it happens, trust me. You also want to make sure you have a strategy for celebrating success, as well. Read on to find out how to deal with both outcomes.

Practical Positive Potty Training

~ 11 ~

WHAT TO DO WHEN THERE'S AN ACCIDENT

It's happening. Everything was going great until, all of a sudden, you see something trickling down your child's leg and onto your carpet. Or your child comes up to you and points down there.

What now?

We've already spoken about the need to stay calm during an accident. I can't stress how important this is, both for your child's wellbeing and your own. Stop and say this with me: accidents are going to happen. You know how I can be so sure? Because the first accident doesn't even really count! That's the first teachable moment. So you know you're going to have to deal with at least one accident, and likely many, many more.

There is not a single child in the world who has ever potty trained without an accident. They are important parts of your child's journey to learning this new skill. Think about how they learned to stand, to talk, or to eat—at first they did it really poorly, but then they got better and better. The same will happen with potty training: your child will learn from their accidents and mistakes.

Set The Tone

Use the first accident as an opportunity to set the tone for the entire potty training process. You have the upper hand here. You are expecting this accident. Greet it with a relaxed, no-big-deal air. Transmit to them your surety, let them know that this was all part of the plan with your calm demeanor. Avoid the following knee-jerk reactions:

- Shouting
- Pulling your child (off a sofa, onto a mat, etc)
- Rolling your eyes or expressing exasperation another way

Instead, replace these reactions with the following:

- A calm, steady voice
- A reassuring pat on the back
- Making eye contact with your little one to reassure them

Now, inform your child in a very matter of fact way about what just happened. You need to adapt this to the level of embarrassment or level of upset that your child is showing. If your child seems distraught by what is happening, lay on the comfort. If they don't even realize what is happening, draw their attention to it softly and sympathetically.

Head To The Potty

Before you begin cleaning up the accident, take your child to the potty. It's possible that with the accident they were cut short, and by placing them on the potty you might just catch a bit of success on the tail end of things.

Be Prepared

On a logistical level, you'll need to be prepared to clean up these accidents without going far from your child. Get your selection of cleaning materials suited to both liquid and solid messes ready before you start potty training. Having everything together in one place will make cleanup that much easier, so that you can multitask. Think scrubbing away a bit of a mess while providing emotional support to your child at the same time. That will be your potty training reality. Have everything you need to clean so that cleanup will not be such a big deal.

Be Constant

Here's a hard truth. There may be days where your child has zero success at potty training. I know, it's hard to imagine or think about, but you need to be prepared for this scenario. Be as consistently upbeat as possible. Do not relay your expectations or project them on your child; instead, celebrate any small victories that you can come up with (made it to the bathroom before the accident? Yay!). Turning an accident into a success if at all possible is a great strategy for dealing with them.

The Truth About Accidents

Accidents are normal. They should definitely not be punished. But at the same time, I am not saying that they should be encouraged, either. If your potty training child starts to view them as acceptable or normal, then you may experience some regression or negative outcomes related to that. The worst case scenario would be having to stop potty training and wait a few months before starting again. That's why it's important to walk the line between chastising and letting go. The safest place to be in this instance is, in my opinion, in a teaching mode. Think of yourself as your child's toilet sensei and of using the bathroom as a simple lesson you must teach.

Practical Positive Potty Training

~ 12 ~

WHAT TO DO WITH POTTY SUCCESS

How you treat potty success is just as important as how you treat the accidents. Your response to successes will lay the foundation of your child's motivation. Some children are born with an inner drive to do grown up things, or try new experiences, but most children need a bit of guidance and some external motivation to convince them to take leaps and bounds forward in their development.

As parents, we tend to provide a lot of this motivation without even thinking about it. It's natural for us, as parents, to get excited whenever our children do something new and, in our doting eyes, impressive. The same is true during the potty training process. Some of the celebration of potty success will just flow out of you naturally. Some of it, however, may not come so easily. There will be successes that come right after sloppy accidents, successes that don't necessarily qualify as success in your mind, such as getting to the bathroom in time but not making it into the toilet, successes that you've already celebrated ten times—in other words, your natural motivation may wane.

However, it's important to remember, for your child's sake, that every success should be celebrated. It's likely that your child will not ever tire of these mini cheers, applauses and celebrations. They thrive on them, and so it's up to you to provide them. Here are a few tips on how to do that:

Keep It Real

Whenever possible, try to really feel happy for your child. Kids are nothing if not expert readers of their parents, and they can smell falsehood from a mile away. Look at each success as a step that is bringing your child closer to being an independent user of the toilet, a goal that is truly exciting for parents who have spent two, three or even four years changing diapers. Now that is something to celebrate, right?

Every Child is Different

It's hard to recommend a certain level of excitement or praise across the board. Every child is different, and for some, an all-out celebration every time they go to the bathroom may be frightening or off-putting. For others, a simple "good job" or "way to go" may go right over their heads without an accompanying gesture or small applause. That's why it's important for you to use your parental instincts to judge the most effective way to celebrate your child's successes.

Celebrating with Rewards

Rewards are a great way to celebrate potty training success. I find them to be so effective that I have devoted an entire section to covering the different ways you can incorporate them into potty training. In that section, I also discuss the different forms rewards and positive reinforcement can take.

SECTION FIVE

~

POTTY TRAINING WITH REWARDS

Next to nakedtime, few potty training innovations have proven to be as impactful on the process as a rewards system. What is a potty training rewards system? At its most basic, it is when a parent creates a cause and effect relationship during the potty training process. The cause is, generally, using the toilet. The effect is almost always a physical, tangible reward. This can range from small toys to candy to stickers. If you decide to work with rewards when potty training, take comfort in the knowledge that you are far from alone. Studies show that over 80% of parents use a rewards system when potty training.[ix]

Rewards can be whatever you want, and whatever motivates your child. However, there are a few key things to keep in mind about choosing rewards:

- **They should be immediate.** It's difficult for a young child to conceptualize any future rewards, so immediate rewards have the most effect.
- If it's something new, even better. If the reward is something that your child has never had or doesn't generally have outside of potty training, that's even better. By associating it solely with potty training, the reward becomes more effective in your child's mind.

- Consistency is key. The consistency of the reward dispensation is the most important aspect. It must be very clear in your child's mind to work. Ie, X happens and I get Y. That simple, that straightforward.

In the following chapters, I'll detail some of the most effective rewards systems, which children they may work for, how to put them in place, and when to transition out of them.

~ 13 ~

THE GOLD STANDARD: THE STICKER CHART

This is one of the most popular rewards systems used by parents potty training.

In my experience, I've seen it work well, for the most part. Some children who need more of an immediate return grow tired of the sticker system, but overall it is a great reward and a way to avoid handing out candy or spending money on bunches of toys.

Generally, the sticker chart is used as a reward in and of itself. To make a sticker chart, get a piece of poster board and divide it up in a calendar format, leaving several columns next to each day. Your child can use the stickers you've chosen to place one next to the current date each time they use the bathroom. This chart will allow them to see, in a single place, all the times they have used the bathroom that day, and over the course of their training. Hang the chart somewhere they can see it many times a day—you'll be surprised at the amount of motivation this can provide for a child, not to mention the boost to their confidence it gives.

Practical Positive Potty Training

If you find yourself with a child who doesn't seem very excited by the compilation of stickers, you can tweak the sticker chart method to give a bit more incentive. In this scenario, a certain number of stickers will get your child a prize. For example, every time they earn five stickers, they can pick out a toy that costs five dollars or less. Or every time they earn seven stickers, they get a special privilege around the house.

~ 14 ~

GAMIFY IT!

Turning potty training into a game is a surefire way to get a kid who is ready to give up back into the groove. This route is a great option for children that simply aren't very excited by the prospect of a sticker, don't particularly like candy, or whose attention span is just too short. Gamification is a proven way to help focus interest on a task in general, and it makes sense that it also works for children potty training.

A Game For Boys

Due to anatomical differences, potty training can be livened up quite a bit for boys. It's important to walk the line between gamifying the act of going to the bathroom and keeping it about doing business, though, to prevent any unwanted sprays.

A fun way to help your boy stand up and use the potty is by placing a small disposable object, like a Cheerio, into the pot. Tell him to aim at the Cheerios while he's using the restroom, and if he hits them, he gets a prize.

Hang It Up

This idea is part game, part arts-and-crafts project. Purchase or cut out a door hanger from a piece of cardboard. Gather up any scraps of paper, fabric, sparkles, pipe cleaners: anything you have laying around. Decorate the 'Potty Hanger' with your child and let them write their name on it. Now, tell them they get to hang it on the door as a sign when they have to use the restroom. For many kids, using something they just made is a great motivation.

The Happy Potty Jar

I love this one, but mostly because it's fun for the adult to participate in, too. Using pieces of paper or even popsicle sticks, write something fun on each one that you and your child can do easily. Some examples could be play outside, watch their favorite movie AGAIN, make ice cream, etc. Each time your child is able to use the potty, they get to draw a little piece of happiness. The surprise element in this game is strong and often motivates children who otherwise are slow to get excited.

A Magic Potty

While not exactly a game, per se, a magic potty sure can seem like one to a child. There are potty training stickers currently on the market that allow children to magically change the color or make an image appear when they wet the sticker. Usually running around $10 to $15, these stickers are easy to use. Place a blank sticker in the bowl of your child's portable potty. When they go to the bathroom in the potty, an image appears slowly on the surface of the sticker. They are available in everything from trucks to butterflies! Once the potty is cleaned and dried, the image disappears and is ready to go again.

~ 15 ~

OTHER FORMS OF REWARDS

Beyond sticker charts and games, the old-fashioned tit-for-tat method is still widely used. This form of reward is a this-for-that set up, meaning your child uses the bathroom and your child gets an immediate reward. Many parents like this kind of system because it is simple, easy to remember, and requires minimal effort on part of the parent. It can also be very effective.

The M&M Method

This one, favored by many parents for its budget-friendliness, is based on the popular M&M candy. In this reward system, the child gets one M&M for successfully going pee in the potty, and two if they are able to poop in the potty. It's easy to put into place and particularly effective for children that are goal-driven. The downside of the M&M method is that many children become expert manipulators of the system, negotiating up the number of M&Ms by initiating a sort of bathroom boycott. This may not be your child, but it is worth considering whether another form of reward or even just simple praise may be enough for your child to be motivated.

This method is called the M&M method but can be done with any candy. Just be sure to choose a candy that you can dispense several times a day without worrying for your child's health. No candy treat is too small, and remember, your child will (hopefully) be getting rewards many times over the course of the potty training!

Toys

The principle of the toy method is the same as the M&M method: one for one. Should your child not be very motivated by sweets, small, inexpensive toys and trinkets can be substituted. Kids go wild for this one, especially when you wrap the presents up and keep them in a big pile near the toilet

A Model Doll

Drink-and-Wet dolls are interesting toys that can serve as a model for little ones that enjoy doll time. These dolls drink and then pee after. By taking the doll to the bathroom after it drinks, you can show your child how using the potty works in a fun way.

Old-Fashioned Simple Praise

Maybe you're reading this chapter thinking 'That sure seems like a lot of bells and whistles', well, you're right. But it's a big step in a child's development, one which many children have difficulty with. If you have any easygoing child, a goal-oriented child, or a child very excited to use the 'grown-up' potty, however, there is a chance that the most simplest of rewards could work for yours—praise.

Oftentimes, we as adults underestimate the power of praise, both verbal and physical, when it comes to encouraging our children. That includes any of the following:

- Saying 'good job!'
- Hugs
- A high-five
- Applause
- Telling your child how proud you are of them

- Kisses
- Compliments
- & more!

By using these verbal and physical tools, you give your child a reward as real as any piece of candy or toy. The emotion that you convey, your excitement and pride, is a great motivator for many children. It is truly the natural last step in the process: you've taught the behavior; your child has met it; and the consequence of that behavior is praise. That praise becomes positive reinforcement, which creates a cycle of good behavior.

That's not all—this type of motivation is external, but it is also intrinsic. By making the praise and success contingent on your child's behaviors, and the 'reward' into something natural and emotionally healthy, you as a parent are taking steps toward raising a healthy, well-functioning adult. It's important for your child's development to mix your usage of external motivation with intrinsic methods, such as praise. That way, your child learns that it's not just about getting a prize all the time. Not to mention, praise is free! You don't have to pack it, it's always there, and it even makes you feel good to give out.

Beyond The Rewards

One last thing that is useful to remember: all of the rewards and fun don't have to be based simply on peeing in the potty. Depending on how quickly or slowly your child is learning, you can tie them to different parts of the potty training puzzle. For example, you can offer your child a reward for simply getting to the bathroom before going, if they are having a bit of a hard time.

It's also important to offer rewards based on the total potty training picture. If you know there are larger events or toys that your child desires, make them hinge on potty training as a whole. Offer to take them to a local play gym or somewhere equally spectacular by letting them know that you can only go when the diapers are gone. Use a common sense tactic, explaining why diapers would ruin the fun.

These natural consequences are great tools to use to help your child learn cause, effect, and the way of the world.

SECTION SIX

~

POTTY TRAINING PITFALLS

Throughout this book, I've tried to paint a realistic picture of the potty-training process. So far we have looked at different ways of potty training, the basic building blocks, and even how to deal with failure, success, and rewards. What I have told you up to now is all accurate and applicable. But I have been saving the sticky stuff for its very own chapter… so welcome to the chapter on Potty Training Pitfalls! Here, I will warn you about some common mistakes and break down a few myths, so that when you hit a bump in the road, you can find out why right here.

Let's face it, if potty training were easy, there wouldn't be so many books about how to accomplish it, right? Just remember, bumps in the road are normal, and your little one is bound to experience some sort of difficulty when dealing with this enormous change. In this chapter, we'll look at those difficulties and focus in on some of the bigger ones.

Practical Positive Potty Training

~ 16 ~

THE SECOND-DAY RESISTANCE

Whether you are using the standard potty training method or trying your hand at a three-day method, the second-day resistance is real. Think about it: you are a very young child, just learning how the world works. Then, your most trusted companions try to change it all up on you! They try to change one of your most basic daily habits. At first, your interest may be piqued, but if you have even a grain of hesitance, it may express itself in rebelliousness.

This is exactly what happens with some children.

The Second-Day Resistance Is Real

When you're in the thick of things, it's hard to tell how well things are going with potty training. How do you judge progress? By the minute? By the hour? By the day? This makes it very difficult as a parent to get through the common second-day resistance.

As its name suggests, the second-day resistance often happens on the second day of potty training. I hear from so many parents that their children seemed alright with potty training on day one, but they seem to have turned against it by day two.

Why the second day? The first day of potty training is filled with excitement, novelty, and confusion. There may also be an element of beginner's luck. The second day is when reality sets in. Stubborn kids see that this wasn't just a one-time thing; nervous kids see that their routine has been changed forever, and fun-loving kids see that this wasn't just a game. So, sometimes on the second day, the child gives up or rebels. They refuse to potty train, or worse, they keep having accidents despite appearing to be on board.

This resistance is not a sign that your child is unready for potty training. In fact, the truth is far from it. This normal phase just needs to be worked through, and often, a breakthrough is on the horizon. So what is a parent to do?

Assess the Reason for the Resistance

This isn't the easiest situation, but there are some steps you can take. First, check in with yourself. Ask yourself if you are treating this and your child like one more item on the to-do list, or if you are truly tuning into your child and letting them know this is a special time for both of you. If you are letting the pressure show, then that could be one reason your child is rebelling. Children are nothing if not good at reading their parents' spoken and non-spoken emotions. Assess the situation carefully, and be sure to examine your own actions above all.

Secondly, be sure you aren't lecturing. Your job here is to be nothing but encouraging. One of the biggest reasons for resistance is an overly lecturing parent. Kids tend to dig in their heels when they feel a lot of pressure from an authority figure, so be sure to intentionally remove any of that pressure from your mannerisms, tone and word choice.

Also, please note, here we are talking about pee, only. Poo is still a whole different ball game, so don't confuse resistance with inability.

Lastly, don't confuse the second-day resistance with the normal potty training process. Most children need more than just a day to learn to potty train, even if that day was very successful. Second-day resistance is marked with a "No!" attitude or evidence of one.

~ 17 ~

PARENTAL PITFALLS

As is the case with the second-day resistance, oftentimes, sadly, we parents are the ones more to blame for failed potty training. This chapter will give you some of the most common mistakes made by 'rookies' (aren't we all, at least once!) and show you how to avoid them or course-correct after them if you are in the thick of things with your toddler.

Are you guilty of any of the following?

Getting Grossed Out

This happens more than you might think. Perhaps you say "but I'm not grossed out by my child's poop." By the time potty training comes around, it's true that we have all as parents changed our fair share of diapers. You have come face to face with your child's worst poos. I will give you that. However, watching a poop happen, or watching it fall on your kitchen tile, is quite a different animal. You may find yourself reacting in an unexpected way, more put off than you originally imagined you might be.

As parents we have to be careful with our reactions during potty training, because our children see them and can immediately feel their weight. Our children know how to read us better than anyone, so it stands to reason that they can see right through any explanations we may offer up as to why let out a big old "UGH" when they did a number two. Be very careful that you are not letting your child see any feelings of disgust when potty training, as it can lead to insecurity, or to your child deciding to no longer poop or pee, holding it in until an accident is inevitable.

Setting Deadlines

You may ask, why would anyone set a potty training deadline? The very real truth is that some nurseries oblige parents to potty train their children before entering, which means parents (and children) who would have otherwise waited have found themselves with their back up against the wall, having to potty train by a certain date on the calendar.

Here's the issue: potty training on a deadline is a very stressful thing. It adds to the stress you may already be feeling, making things even more difficult than they would have been otherwise. The stress is almost always felt by the child, as well, even if the adult does their best to conceal. High expectations create a lot of pressure on the tiny shoulders of a child. They can end up giving up on the goal, as it can seem out of reach.

If you do have a deadline, such as starting nursery in September, my best advice is to put a false deadline ahead of that time, so that you give yourself and your child some breathing room. This artificial deadline won't produce nearly the amount of stress, but it will give you a date to work toward that can potentially help you reach your real deadline, with no serious consequences.

External Stress

An important question to ask yourself if potty training isn't going as planned: what is going on in my life at the moment? Any source of external stress could be knowingly or unknowingly affecting your behavior. If you are going through a difficult time at work, a time of transition or separation, or dealing with the death of a loved one, give yourself a break and don't try to potty train! Potty training will always be there, and it's important for you to be in the best possible frame of mind for your child. So if there is any identifiable external stressor in your life right now, be sure to take that into account.

Practical Positive Potty Training

~ 18 ~

...AND MORE

There are as many reasons why potty training may not be working as there are children potty training. Here are a handful more that you can run through if you find yourself running out of tricks and ideas.

Potty-Training Boot camp

Potty-training boot camp may sound to you like some sort of new age-y idea invented to cajole money from parents who are too busy to deal with their children. The potty-training boot camp is actually a term that moms use to refer to an intense period of potty training meant to get the job done, fast. The three-day method, which I mentioned earlier, could be categorized as potty-training boot camp.

While this method works wonders for some kids, it's not for all. In the cases where it doesn't work, it can help to get a jump-start on potty training even when the toughest potty training pieces (nap time, nighttime etc.) take longer to fall into place. However, for still other children, it ends up being a negative experience.

The stress of such an intense change is a lot for some kids. That's why potty training boot camp gets a section in the pitfalls chapter. Sometimes, when a child is sensitive or has some sort of trauma around the subject, the boot camp can just be too intense. If you as a parent see that your child is not enjoying themselves, please evaluate if this method is truly working. Do not force the intense potty training method. You may end up leaving a bad association in their minds about the toilet, which will negatively affect any potty training future.

Potty Attachment

For those parents who use a potty chair with their children, you may experience something I like to call 'potty attachment'. This is when your child has (understandably) become very attached to their own potty chair, showing hesitance or unwillingness to use any other potty. It can also take the form of being unwilling to use the big potty when it's time to make the transition, or when you are out and about.

This pitfall is relatively common, and it's easy to understand why. From your child's point of view, the toilet is an enormous, loud contraption with a gaping hole filled with scary water. Unless, that is, you gradually convince them otherwise.

If you are set on using a potty chair but want to be able to overcome your child's fear of other potties, it's very helpful to normalize foreign objects and bathrooms. With your child, point out everything that this new bathroom or the big potty has in common with their favorite potty chair or home bathroom. The sink, the trash can, the mirror....see? It's just like at home. Or the hole, the seat, the water...you get the idea. Explain this brightly and nonchalantly, avoiding any sense of pressure.

Practical Positive Potty Training

The Attack of the Screens

Sometimes we set our children up for failure without meaning to. If you are having a hard time with potty training, be sure to evaluate your child's screen time. The time your child is watching a tablet or the TV is time that they are not very tuned in to their bodily functions. Think about it—how many times have you seen your child turn into a zombie when watching a show or a movie? It's not the most conducive atmosphere for potty training, and your child is far from an expert. They need all their faculties to be able to discern when they have to go, until that becomes a habit.

Holding It In

A very common occurrence during potty training, holding in pee, or more commonly poop, can be caused by a multitude of things. Not wanting to poop in the potty can quickly progress to not wanting to poop at all, or poop withholding. It can be stressful as a parent, and can even be physically harming for the child. The reasons behind holding it in range from a battle of wills, a fear of poop or the toilet, or a physical limitation such as constipation. So how do you deal with holding it in?

First, get yourself in a very patient mindset. No one likes to be rushed when pooping, and pressure to poo can definitely have the opposite effect. It's great to get into a routine, such as trying to poop 15 minutes after a meal. Oftentimes, the movement of the bowels as the digestive process cranks up is enough to give your little one that extra push they need to poo.

Read books about pooping. Colorful, illustrated books about going poop take out any fear that your little one may be feeling about the issue. They make pooping more familiar, and even fun! Also, evaluate your child's diet. Perhaps it's time to add a few fiber-rich foods to their lunch tray? Or you may want to include natural laxatives, such as prunes. These times can feel desperate, so be sure to give yourself permission to allow your child to poop in comfort. If that means giving in and allowing them to use the little potty again, it may be a good idea. Anything to get the pooping back on track, and you can course correct later.

Practical Positive Potty Training

~ 19 ~

IT'S JUST NOT WORKING

Maybe you have read through all the possible pitfalls and none of them really fit. Or perhaps you are sensing a lot of constant resistance from your little one. As much as I hate to say it, it may be time to throw in the towel. But don't worry! I'm only talking about a temporary reprieve. Don't think about it as giving up; think about it as a reschedule.

The False Start and the Reset

Sometimes a parent can misread their child's readiness and commence potty training too soon. How do you know if this is the case with you? If you are meeting with total resistance, over a prolonged period of several days, this could be the case. If you are feeling at your wit's end, and like you just can't handle the exhaustion and the frustration, this could be the case. Should you identify with this, I have some good news.

Practical Positive Potty Training

It's not too late to start over.

I give you full permission to throw in the towel, pull back out the diapers, and patiently wait for another window of readiness. It is not the end of the world, and it will end up saving you loads of headache and will help to keep your child's outlook on potty training positive.

In the interim, be sure not to talk about potty training more than in a natural way if it happens to come up in conversation. Do not make comparison comments or point out how good other children are doing. Call it off and prepare for The Reset, as my fellow potty training expert Jamie Glowacki calls this fresh start.[x]

The steps to a successful reset are the following:

1. On the evening of the day you decide to rediaper, put all the potty training paraphernalia back in its box and tuck it away in a closet somewhere.
2. Diaper your child for their bedtime (never during a potty training tantrum).
3. Tell your child what is happening. You can say something as simple as "You are not doing your business on the potty, so we are going to put a diaper on you again."
4. Aim for a Reset that lasts for less than a month. A good minimum time to reset is two weeks, as that gives your child enough time to 'forget' most of the bad associations they may have formed.
5. Do not lecture your child at any moment.
6. Use the time to calm down, gain perspective, and prepare for your next round of potty training. Choose a date and start thinking positive. When the date is looming, you can mention it offhandedly to your child.

There's just one caveat here: some children will ask about their potty, but not for it. That's fine. However, a few children may ask to use the potty. If your child does this, and uses it properly, thank them and let them know that if they continue to use it, it can stay out, but if they don't use it properly, it will be put back up.

The only child for whom I do not recommend a Reset is the child older than three. For a child under two, the Reset may not count as a full reset, and could actually just be a case of your child being a bit unaware still of the idea of potty training. Just chalk it up to them being too young and pay extra attention to decide when to start again.

It's Just a Regression

If your child seemed to be fully potty trained and suddenly starts having multiple accidents, you may have a regression on your hands. A major transition could be the cause, like if a new child is being welcomed to the household or school has just started.

Regressions can happen anywhere from a week into potty training to months after a successful potty training. They can happen in the form of multiple accidents, or they can also take the form of your child asking to put on a diaper again. In the latter case, you have the choice of humoring them—after all, their request for a diaper may just be another form of dress-up. It's likely they will go back to using the bathroom in no time.

Many cases of regression are an expression of the desire for attention. Therefore, the best solution is to be sure you are giving your child your full attention when you are sharing quality time together. Tell them you love them even more than you already do. If the cause for the regression seems to be a new or younger sibling, emphasize how big and how skilled your older child is. They'll never get tired of hearing it, and often we don't say it nearly enough. Think of each compliment, each I love you, and each moment you spend together as adding up in their little hearts like a bank account. Allow them to recharge every now and again, and it may help solve the regression.

Many regressions go away on their own after a few weeks, so take heart and keep on going.

Practical Positive Potty Training

SECTION SEVEN

~

POTTY TRAINING IN OTHER CULTURES

People from other countries and cultures potty train their children differently than in the United States. While we all poop, as the saying goes, how we learn to do it is not necessarily the same.

Babies born in the U.S. most often wear disposable diapers from birth to around ages two or three. Some parents opt for cloth diapers for a good chunk of their baby's time pre-potty trained.

Once it's time to potty train, parents in the United States tend to fall back on their roots to guide them through the process. For example, white American children start potty training later than Black American children. When researched, African-American children start potty training around 18 months of age, whereas white children start training closer to 24 months on average.

Other countries and cultures use a variety of different items for diapering purposes and sometimes nothing at all. On top of that, how old their children are when they start to toilet train varies greatly.

It's been noted that the farther away from the equator you travel, the later in age children are to be fully potty trained. According to Dr. Sydney Spiesel, professor of pediatrics at Yale University's School of Medicine, studies have shown that the average age of toilet training around the world seems to be directly proportional to the latitude. Climate seemingly has a great deal to do with the reasoning. The colder the temperatures, the longer children stay in diapers.

~ 20 ~

HOW IT'S DONE ACROSS THE WORLD

Every culture has quirks and differences when it comes to potty training. It's fascinating to learn about the differences, especially as a parent in the thick of potty training. There may be some bits and pieces that you'd like to pick out and use in your own child's potty-training journey. One thing's for certain—although each culture does this differently, it's clear that each culture's way works about the same, bringing us back to the key to remember when potty training—everybody eventually gets potty trained.

Turkey

In Turkey, many children are draped in cloth diapers. Depending on the amount of education the mother has and the socioeconomic differences, many children are potty trained when they are over the age of 18 months. Statistically, it takes an average of seven months to get them out of diapers.

Kenya

A group of Digo people in Msambweni, Kenya was watched and interviewed in 1977. Researchers noted that these East African mothers started toilet training their babies within the first month of life. By the age of six months, most babies were found to be completely potty trained.

How is this possible?

Mothers carefully watched their baby's food and liquid intake. They learned their baby's behaviors and habits. If the mother thought that her baby had to pee, she would sit on the ground, with her legs straight out in front of her, and place the baby between her legs. The baby would be faced away from the mother, near her knees. Then the mother would make a "shuus" or hissing noise and wait for the infant to urinate. The infant was then rewarded for peeing during the sound. The child was expected to urinate in position and on command, at the latest, by four to five months, according to the researchers.

Pooping was taught in a similar fashion. The babies would sit facing their mother. The infant's knees would be placed over the mother's ankles, one leg over each of the mothers. This created a straddling position for the baby, but they were supported by the mother's feet. As the mother helped support their infant, they would make noises that simulated the sounds one would make when having a bowel movement. If the baby pooped, it would be rewarded.

The Digo are simple people with few luxuries. They don't have furnished homes or long rides to work. They live simple lives with family members assisting in raising their children. They work together to farm and live off the land. As the saying goes, "It takes a village to raise a child." The Digo people are exemplary models of this phrase.

Israel

In Israel, children who attend childcare are potty trained together. The toddlers are lined up and placed in front of a toilet. The children are then rewarded with praise and encouragement should they pee or poop in the toilet. Those who do not use the potty are more likely to use the potty the next time the toddlers are all lined up.

China

Chinese babies are potty trained very young, much like the Digo people. Babies begin potty training when they are just a few months old. They are held over a toilet, or by the edge of the road, while their mother makes peeing sounds. By the age of six months, most children are potty trained.

To facilitate the use of a toilet, or void when they need to, Chinese babies and toddlers wear open-crotched pants called kaidangku. This traditional clothing allows children to urinate and defecate freely without soiling their clothes. By the time the toddlers are a year old, they know how to squat down wherever they are to pee or poop. This garment remains the pants style of choice for toddlers living in the Chinese countryside.

It has been thoroughly documented that Chinese children, especially those raised in poorer communities, will squat and defecate wherever they are, whether it's on a public sidewalk or public transportation. These actions are not frowned upon; they are culturally acceptable.

Cote D'Ivoire

Located on the Ivory Coast of Africa, west of Nigeria, lives a community called the Beng people. These folks have a very different way of potty training their children. Within days of the baby's arrival, Beng women administered enemas twice as day, starting after the umbilical stump has fallen off. By the time the baby is a few months old, they're trained to not poop at all during the day.

The Beng villages are quite poor, and babies spend most of the day strapped to a caregiver's back as they work in the fields. As a culture, the Beng people consider feces to be disgusting. Being a baby still does not give someone the right to poop on another member of the community. A caregiver would refuse to watch a baby who poops on them, so mothers ensure that the baby's colon is emptied before they leave home for the day. The baby is "trained" to not poop during the day because its body gets into a routine of being cleaned early each morning.

Germany

Potty training, prior to the country's unification, was done differently in East and West Germany.

In East Germany, potty training was a social experience, where potty benches are used. These were exactly what they sound like; toddlers sat on the bench at the same time and were expected to pee and poop together.

There were strict guidelines how the German Democratic Republic (GDR) raised their children. Eating, playing, and pooping together were noted in rules.

Folks in West Germany blamed the potty training efforts for many personality traits of the Eastern. In 1999 German criminologist Professor Christian Pfeiffer alleged that forced potty training broke a child's naturally rebellious spirit.

Today, potty training in Germany is much more lax. Boys and girls are taught to sit on the potty to learn how to pee. This is so that boys don't have to try to pee, aim, balance, and think all at the same time. They are also left in the nude if it helps to facilitate potty training. The fewer clothes in the way, the better.

Many German children are potty trained in the spring and summer, so that clothing, even outside, is not a necessity. People don't seem to care as it's socially acceptable for a child to be playing outdoors in the nude. The toddlers are also not rushed to potty train. Germans don't expect their children to learn to use the potty right away, and it's true that when they can squat next to any tree to relieve themselves, why should they be hurried. As long as they are learning when they need to go, it's more important than where they actually go.

Vietnam

Vietnamese babies start toilet training very early and are typically potty trained by nine months of age. In their culture, much like those of Kenya, diapers are rarely used. Again, the mothers use whistling sounds to trigger their child to urinate. They watch their children closely to learn the signs of a need to pee or poop. By the age of 24 months most all Vietnamese children are completely potty trained, and many did it with little assistance from their parents. It is said that the technique actually strengthens the bladders of Vietnamese babies quickly, and they are able to control the urination process faster and more effectively.

Netherlands

Dutch children have been monitored for many years around the topic of potty training. Current literature includes a study completed in 1996 which is often compared to a similar one conducted in 1966. Children were found to be potty trained between the ages of one and five.

Boys were found to be potty trained around the age of three years old. Girls trained a little sooner, and were completely potty trained by around two and a half.

The type of diaper used was found to play a big part in the age at which a child was potty trained. Interestingly, children tended to potty train much earlier in 1966 than they did in 1996. The presence of other children in the house, attending day care, and the age at which children start walking all had positive correlations with the data sets.

England

A study conducted in the United Kingdom in 2009 revealed an interesting finding about the age at which children were potty trained and problems maintaining dryness throughout the day and night.

Toddlers who were trained later than 24 months of age were found to have more problems controlling their bladders around the clock. The report concluded that delaying the onset of toilet training until after two years prolongs the exposure time to potential stressors that could interfere with bladder control. The findings did not change regardless of the child's gender, any known developmental delays, or if the mother reported postpartum depression.

Palestine

In some Palestinian territories, parents begin potty training at around 15 months of age, since most don't work outside of the home. In the case of working women, children are potty trained closer to age two.

Indonesia

Indonesia is not a wealthy country, and for that reason, diapers are generally too expensive for most parents to utilize. Toddlers typically urinate wherever they are standing. Most children are toilet trained early on to use either a squat toilet, a ditch, or defecate beside a rice field. The term "potty training" isn't even in most people's vocabulary in Indonesia.

Toilet paper is also a luxury in Indonesia. In fact, you will be hard pressed to find a roll of toilet paper, even in tourist destinations. Bathrooms that have a squat or seated toilet typically have a bucket of water nearby. Hand placement is important. With your right hand you grab a ladle filled with water from the bucket. You then pour water into your left hand and use the water to wipe.

While this may seem unusual for Americans, it is fairly common is Southeast Asian countries. In fact, the Association of Southeast Asian Nations (ASEAN) was established in August 1967 and governs what bathrooms must have in them.

The member states of ASEAN include Brunei Darussalam, Cambodia, Indonesia, Laos , Malaysia, Myanmar, Philippines, Singapore, Thailand, and Vietnam.

According to literature published by ASEAN, public toilets are "a room or booth shared by all people at all times for urination and defecation consisting of at least a bowl fitted with or without a seat (seating or squatting) and connected to a waste pipe and a flushing apparatus. This standard also focuses on public toilets frequented by tourists at places of interest/transit points/popular shopping areas." As for those who live outside of tourist destinations, citizens simply go to the bathroom wherever is most convenient.

And…The United States

While it is obvious that people around the world potty train their children in many different ways, in the United States we typically start our children on either a toilet seat or a smaller potty seat, as was covered in Chapter 3. Where some techniques work best for their families, in their households, and in their countries, Americans are accustomed to flush toilets and toilet paper. We are also used to utilizing disposable diapers, or cloth diapers at the very least. While our children aren't potty trained as infants, or by the age of one, all children, unless they have a medical condition, are typically potty trained before the age of four.

SECTION EIGHT

~

POTTY TRAINING ALL TYPES OF CHILDREN

No child is the same. That is the beauty of procreating, the beauty of being a parent, and the beauty of life. It also makes things a tiny bit difficult when you are navigating the different phases of childhood. It is quite difficult to predict how a child will react before the task of potty training. Not every child will succumb to the generally effective methods of potty training that are outlined in the book. And even if the rewards system, the three-day training, and the other tricks and types of potty training *do* work on your child, there are unique tips and quirks that are useful to know about for every type of child, be it a boy, girl, demanding, special needs, or distracted one.

Read on in this section as I cover the different types of children and how you can adjust potty training to be more effective for them.

~ 21 ~

POTTY TRAINING GIRLS

While the world of gender is more fluid than ever nowadays, the fact remains that the male and female anatomy are quite different. It is also a fact that there are different tricks and tips that can help with the average little girl that do not apply to the average little guy. That's why in this and the next chapter, I wanted to spend time covering boys and girls separately.

When Are Girls Ready?

There is no hard-and-fast rule about when children are ready to potty train. However, one recurring truth is that girls are consistently ready to potty train earlier than boys. On average, girls are potty trained three months before boys. Though it is true that children are so different, and your girl could just as easily wait until she is four to potty train, statistically she is likely to train before her brother. One survey of over 1000 parents[xi] showed that 54% of them started potty training with their girl before the age of two, while only 38% of parents started their boy potty training before two years old.

What Is It Called?

This may seem like a funny question, but it's one of those logistical things that parents often don't think about until they're in the moment. What will you call your daughter's private parts?

The main goal is to be natural. You want to choose a word that can roll off your tongue comfortably. However, you also may want to be aware that there will be a moment in your daughter's life when she uses that word in public. How will it be received? I recommend choosing a word that won't cause her embarrassment or make her feel out of place.

Some parents are more technical. Some mothers use different language than fathers. Some are silly. Which are you? Here are some words people use as alternatives to vagina:

- Front bottom
- Fanny
- Titi
- Flower
- Tutu
- Lady business
- Foo foo
- Cootchie

Mastering The Wipe

With a girl, the most important teachable moment is the wipe. Girls are generally more prone to urinary tract infections than boys, and at this age things are no different. It is important to teach your daughter the best way to wipe, from front to back. Wiping from front to back prevents germs from entering the bladder. This will help prevent infections and create healthy habits for your daughter.

Spraying Urine

If you thought boys were the only ones who missed the toilet—think again. Girls have been known to spray urine, especially when they are not positioned in an ideal way. When little girls sit far back on the potty seat, they may spread their legs too wide to steady themselves. This can cause the urine to shoot outward. To solve the problem, just get your daughter to move her legs closer together, so they are pointing outward from the potty, so that her urine goes down into the toilet.

What To Wear

When toilet training girls, there is an easy wardrobe solution, especially for when you have to leave the house yet still need easy access for bathroom purposes. Dresses, for obvious reasons, make great potty training clothes. Your daughter won't have to pull any pants down, undo any buttons, or unzip anything on her way to the toilet. It's a good idea not to use very long dresses, however, and also to teach her to tuck the front edge of the dress into the neck, so it doesn't end up hanging in the water or getting soaked in urine.

Let Her Help You Pick It Out

Most girls take, especially, to being able to pick out their potty-training accessories. The act of choosing something they like makes them excited for this journey, more likely to stick with it, and helps them to feel like a big girl. Cute training pants, with favorite figures and colors, can work wonders and really get them excited to use the bathroom. The same goes with the actual potty. It just helps to smooth over the transition and the process, making it easier for everyone.

Practical Positive Potty Training

~ 22 ~

POTTY TRAINING BOYS

Now it's time to tackle potty training little boys, and the nuances that make this process slightly different. Anatomically, there's no denying that potty training boys is quite a different ball game. However, it's not just the difference in genitalia that changes the game. Boys have a different developmental cycle, and they also often feature different personality traits that makes this a very different process.

When Are Boys Ready?

This is the moment when we face the cold, hard truth: girls are more "on it" than boys. The majority of boys show a readiness to potty train around age two and a half. It is important to note that every child is an individual, and it's completely possible that your boy may show interest and readiness as early as 18 months, so you need to be sure to observe closely and look for signs mentioned in previous chapters.

What Is It Called?

You may have already hit this milestone moment: deciding what to call your son's penis. Usually, little boys become aware of their anatomy around age one, when they discover and play with themselves when changing and bathing. So what do you call your son's private parts?

The most important thing is to be natural. You should choose a word you are comfortable with. If penis seems too scientific or technical, you can choose another term to call it. It should be as natural as saying stomach, elbow, and arm. There's nothing wrong with choosing an alternate name—just make sure it's something that won't embarrass your child when he says it for the first time in public. Just as some parents prefer to say pee instead of urine and poo instead of feces, you can choose a nickname for your son's privates, starting with the list below:

- Pee pee
- Wee wee
- Willy
- Winky
- Weiner
- Ding-dong
- Ding-a-ling
- Thing

The Bath Pee

One of my favorite ways to practice and build up excitement around potty training is to create a game around peeing in the bath. If that doesn't sound sanitary to you, then it's important to note that all children pee in the bath, whether you make a game out of it, whether you recognize it, or whether you want it. It's just their natural response when they get wet and relaxed.

The main goal here is to call his attention to when he is peeing. You can accomplish that with a simple "Hey, you're peeing, awesome!" This is the perfect time to do so as it's obvious when your child is going.

The game is nothing more than holding a small plastic cup out to catch pee. This will help him connect the idea of what is coming out of him with the fact that he can control it. He may even start to tell you when he feels he is about to pee. Encourage him to try to aim at the cup, to see if he can land any inside. And remember, it's a game! It won't have any instant effect, but it will prepare your son by sharpening individual skills he needs to be successfully potty trained.

Boy Accessories

There are a couple of accessories that are boy-specific. The one that may be worth your time is the mini-urinal. Potty training boys is a messy business, and regular little potties aren't enough to protect your bathroom or hallway walls from an aim that hasn't quite been honed. That's where the mini-urinal may be useful. If you have already started teaching your boy to pee standing up, these urinals will stop any major splashes, a better option than a traditional low potty-training seat or the big toilet. They tend to have tall backs, giving them a throne-like appearance.

Dad, The Starring Role

There's no doubt that when potty training a boy, dads have the upper hand. Being male and sharing an anatomy is not an essential part of potty training a son, but it is generally quite helpful. Learning by example is the best way to learn, so it only makes sense that by watching his father use the bathroom, your son will learn more quickly how to go. He can watch his father's form, watch him stand, aim, shake, and finish the job.

Dad can be good for more than just modeling behavior, though. Potty training a son can actually be a bonding experience for parents. I have friends who gave their wives the weekend "off" with her friends and set up a potty-training camp of sorts by covering seats and sofas with plastic, introducing big-guy underwear, and hanging out in said underwear all weekend. Every hour on the hour they would play a game to see who could pee, and overall the experience was relaxing and a great bonding opportunity.

Peeing Standing Up

This is a fairly important moment for boys, and one that has no analogous moment for girls. This is the moment when you teach your son to pee standing up. Some parents skip straight from diapers to standing up, but I recommend passing by the peeing-sitting-down stage first. That way you have paved the road a bit for pooping as well as peeing.

So how do you make the transition to standing? The best way is for your son to see a role model in action. Seeing his brother, father, grandfather, or friends stand up is a surefire way for him to learn to do it himself. If your son is reluctant, don't force it—allow him to pee sitting down until he shows a bit of initiative, which usually doesn't take longer than a week. The Cheerios method, outlined earlier, in which your son tries to aim and hit Cheerios in the toilet, is a great trick. I've found in most cases, a little lighthearted fun like this is all it takes for your child to get excited about peeing standing up.

Hygiene

When teaching your boy to pee standing up, you'll also want to incorporate hygiene and safety practices into your teaching—for your sanity and for his future caregiver's and even wife's sanity, too! The basic steps to standing peeing up should be the following:

- Lifting up the seat
- Wiping up spills and splashes
- Putting the seat down

Try to convey to your child that these are normal parts of peeing, just as essential as unzipping his pants or even washing his hands.

~ 23 ~

POTTY TRAINING CHILDREN WITH SPECIAL NEEDS

So many books and blogs that feature potty-training recommendations are created with the "average" child in mind. Average is in quotes here because I'm not even sure what an average child is. Every child, yours, mine, and all the others in between, is different. They meet milestones at different times. They react differently to different stimuli. They find motivation in different places. However, children with special needs can present a unique challenge when it comes to potty training. Whether theirs is a disability, ADHD, or another challenge, a special needs child often has special rules that apply when potty training. In this chapter, I'll look at a few of those to help parents of special needs kids along the way.

Physical Disability

For children with a physical disability, potty training can present some unique challenges. However, the truth is so many of the tips and ideas we've been going over are still important when potty training special needs children. Potty training is a very custom-fitted process, so that works in favor of parents with a special needs child.

There are a few things to keep in mind when potty training a child with a physical disability:

- Take some time to get the best potty or adapter for your child and their special needs. Think padded seats, rails, back support—whatever their situation calls for, and whatever will make them comfortable on the toilet.
- Take some extra time to try to figure out their elimination pattern. When nakedtime isn't an option, or things are harder to access, having an idea of the "danger" zones can be the difference between a successful potty-training routine and failure.
- Consider a bidet. There are bidet adapters that can be fitted on a regular toilet, and they can help children with limited range of motion cleanup.
- Consider your child's mood. Keep them happy while in the bathroom, catering to their needs and even singing a favorite song to make sure that being in the bathroom is a pleasant experience.
- Do your research on any side effects that your child's medications may have, so you can take the proper steps to counteract them.

Learning Disabilities

Learning disabilities don't only affect children in the classroom, they can cause issues when learning life skills, too. As a parent to a learning-disabled child, it's likely you already have superhuman patience. That's great because this is the perfect time to exercise it.

I recommend starting a bit later with children in this category as they can find a start-and-stop experience very off-putting to potty training. It's important to keep it all as low stakes as possible and recognize that it will likely take a longer time to potty train your special needs baby.

Diabetes

A small note for any diabetic children: children with type 1 diabetes may urinate more frequently than other kids, and thereby need more hydration. It is important to maintain an eye on your child in this case, especially on their state of well-being, as that will be the best indicator as to whether something is wrong.

Hypospadius

This is a fancy word for a fairly common "defect" in which the hole of the penis is on the underside of the member. Most children have this corrected when they are young. However, if your child has been diagnosed with this or you suspect he may have it, he will likely need to pee sitting down.

~ 24 ~

POTTY TRAINING DIFFERENT CHILDREN

Sometimes, the difference in potty training comes not from gender or from disability but from a simple difference in personality. Do you know your child? Some kids are totally goal driven. Others are stubborn to the core, a potentially very difficult personality to potty train. It doesn't really matter which type of child you have—the most important step is to potty train that child. Don't waste your time wishing you had an "easier" child or taking steps that "should" work. Potty training is all about flexibility on your part, being able to adapt and craft the process to your child's reactions. It's not the time to fix any behavioral problems; it's time to embrace your child's unique behaviors and use them, if possible, to your advantage.

The "I'm Bored" Kid

If your child is one of those who is always flitting from game to game, losing interest quickly, you may have an "I'm Bored" kid on your hands. This type also often applies to the very smart child, the one who is independent and finds his own entertainment piddling with mechanical toys or building dollhouses from the ground up. With this child, it's important to keep potty training logical, quick, and nimble. Use a reward they really like, and the most likely is that you will find a very responsive toddler indeed.

The Scaredy Cat

Some kids are just more timid and fearful than others. Sometimes, as an adult, it's hard to understand these fears. Potty training, for most of us, was such a long time ago that we simply can't recall what it was that seemed so frightening. However, faced with change, plus a difficult new skill, your child may feel very real fear.

A great way to get your scaredy cat child to start using the potty is to put them at the wheel. This flips the dynamic upside down, switching the focus from "Am I afraid of this?" to "I am in charge." One fun way to do this is to put your child in charge of teaching their favorite stuffed animal how to use the bathroom. Go through all the steps—your child should teach their stuffed animal to put on underpants, give them rewards, and everything in between. This will help reinforce the idea that your child knows how to do this, and that it's not a scary thing.

Many children don't have a problem with peeing but do get scared when it comes to pooping. I've seen children who would rather use the bathroom in their underwear than poop in the toilet. The best thing you can do here is make sure that your child is getting plenty of fiber and liquid, as that will allow them to remain as regular as possible despite their fear of using the toilet.

The Younger Child

Are you starting potty training before your child turns two? There are positives to this approach. Younger children are very adaptable, and they still love to feel your approval and know they are doing something that pleases you. However, the fact that they are still connected to you and dependent on you for certain things is a double-edged sword. If you start with a younger child, you may have to help them each time they go to the bathroom.

The Older Child

Are you starting potty training later, such as after your child is three and a half or four? That can be challenging due to your child's newfound will. They may be anxious to exercise all their independence and willpower against any plan you propose. This resistance is often the most difficult road bump for those who wait later to potty train. I encourage parents of strong-willed children to try to get on the earlier end of potty training rather than waiting later.

One of the keys to potty training the older child is making sure that you have their permission. Ask your child before you begin, and make sure you get a yes. Try to remain as nonchalant as possible as you don't want to add any pressure to the process.

Practical Positive Potty Training

SECTION NINE

~

POTTY TRAINING: IT'S A PROCESS

As you have probably gathered from this book, potty training is a process. There will be bumps in the road, and there may even be U-turns. But keep going, reaching for wins, even if they are small. Some of these bumps along the road are perfectly normal. The children that transition neatly from diapers to not wetting the bed at night are nearly nil. In this chapter, we will look at some of the biggest bumps as you continue the process toward a 100% potty-trained child. Read on to find out how to deal with nights, bed-wetting, leaving your house (because some day you may want to, ha!) and even how to know that you've done it!

~ 25 ~

IN THE STILL OF THE NIGHT

Everyone talks about how to potty train during the day. But obviously the night is important, too, and for a child to be totally potty trained, they need to be able to make it through the daytime and the nighttime without accidents. So how do you go about night training? In this chapter, I'll break it down for you and answer your burning questions.

The Myths About Night Training

Night training should not be about withholding liquids and waking up your sleeping child. I see so many parents jump through crazy hoops trying to do anything to get their child to get through the night without wetting the bed, but the truth is, it just takes time. Generally, children take about two to four months after potty training to night train. That's the bottom line. bed-wetting is a totally normal occurrence. And waking up your child to pee several times throughout the night is likely to cause more headache than to bring you any closer to a consistently dry night and a child who knows how to accomplish that. So how do you help lead your child to a dry night?

When to Do It

First, you need to decide whether to try simultaneous day and night training or to focus on them separately. As I mentioned earlier, the normal thing is for a child to master daytime training and then nighttime. However, I wanted to point out that there are those who tackle both at the same time. It is a personal decision, but I will mention that if you want to tackle this simultaneously, you will likely need to employ exterior forces, such as a night pee schedule in which you wake up your child (and, hence, must be woken up yourself). If you decide to let dryness be your guide and allow your child to organically fall into sleep potty training, you may find that it's just a matter of time and you didn't have to bend over backward to make it happen. Most kids naturally stop wetting the bed at night after being potty trained. A good limit for parents who would like to allow it to develop naturally but are wondering when it will happen is the following: if your child has not stopped wetting the bed by three and a half years, it's a good idea to use further techniques to help them do so.

Prepare the Bed

It's important to get the bed prepared for accidents. Because for a month, maybe two, maybe more, you are going to be dealing with wet nights and spontaneous accidents. You will be surprised how much peace of mind you gain from covering your child's mattress with plastic, preparing a few extra sets of bedsheets, and getting your mind in the right place. Knowing that you will be washing sheets a few times a week really takes the annoying, surprise factor out of things, which in turn helps you not overreact with your child. This should not be frustrating for you or your child—it is natural.

Night Naked Time

How does night training work? Essentially, by your child feeling the wetness around them. I find that Pull-Ups or other nighttime diaper-like aids are counterproductive. Yes, they keep the bed clean. But they do so by eliminating one of our best tools for teaching night training: uncomfortable wetness. Like it or not, the feeling of lying in their own wetness is the alarm and the motivator for children at night. The power of night diapers means that your child stays dry and feeling wonderful—a nice tool when they are newborns, struggling to find their rhythm, but not quite as desirable when you want them to learn to get up and go to the bathroom. That's why I recommend using either big kid underwear, no underwear (just pyjamas) or even going bottomless. This is how you will get your child to feel what is going on, and they should little by little wake up sooner and realize what is going on, which will lead to a fully trained child before too long.

Getting Started

Once you have prepared the bed, it's time to communicate what is happening with your child. Explain to them why they aren't wearing diapers or underwear. Make it clear that this is another new phase in life, one in which there will be different actions and moments that you will be tackling together.

Tell your child that they are big enough to stop wetting the bed at night. Tell them that, as they learn, it is perfectly normal for them to wet the bed, and (this is key) show them what to do when they have wet the bed. At this point, I don't recommend limiting liquids as much as trying to phase out the liquids taken right before your child sleeps. If they are accustomed to drinking milk before bed, reduce the amount as you simultaneously add it in at another time in their evening schedule. As long as you do so little by little, your child shouldn't put up too much resistance.

I recommend teaching your child to put a thick blanket or towel over the wet part and then go back to sleep. Then remind them every time you tuck them in, emphasizing how big they are and how proud you will be if they don't have an accident or are able to deal with it by themselves. When they almost certainly come wake you up, just remind them what they should do, and show them yourself. I strongly believe this is the most painless way forward for most children. With time, they will simply learn not to wet the bed at night.

If It Doesn't Work

Fortunately, there is an invention that I have seen great results from for those who haven't been able to night train their children by age three and a half. The bed-wetting alarm is just what it sounds like, a device that goes off (in a non-scary way) when it senses wetness in the bed. A child using the bed-wetting alarm wakes themselves up upon hearing the alarm, and eventually they begin to wake up sooner and sooner, before stopping bed-wetting altogether. Keep that one in your back pocket just in case. They are available online and in stores like Babies R Us.

~ 26 ~

CONTINUING ON THE ROAD OF POTTY TRAINING

Apart from night training and bed-wetting, which is the major hurdle on the road to complete potty training, there are other common bumps. In this chapter, we'll go over the ones most likely to trip you up.

After the Intensive Potty Training

After you've gone through the intensive potty training, whether it was three days or whether you are headed into week two, you'll likely find that a change in strategy is necessary. If your child hasn't gotten potty training down pat yet, you may need to try a new strategy, or at the very least tweak your old one.

It is common that children who haven't mastered potty training at the first go-round show some resistance to the idea of potty training. Oftentimes, this resistance rears its head when your child is otherwise occupied. A prime example of this is screen time. If you allow your child screen time, they are very likely to release bladder control when they are in the thick of one of their favorite episodes. The solution? A simple rule. Screen time comes after potty time. That's it. No discussion, no bending, just a simple boundary for your child to follow.

The same resistance can come at other times when your child is very involved or seated for a long time—think mealtimes, car rides, or playtime. The solution is the same, create the boundary and present it to your toddler. Call it "our rule"; insist on a bathroom trip before meals and long sitting sessions, and be consistent.

When You're Not At Home

Potty training away from home can fill a parent's heart with dread. But it doesn't have to. There are ways to set you and your child up for success. That said, I do recommend trying not to venture out at all the first week of potty training, and only for very short bursts the second and/or third week.

Before venturing out, be sure that your child is consistently able to anticipate their urge to go to the bathroom and tell you. Make sure they are comfortable sitting on a toilet. I also recommend waiting until they have returned to full clothing (if you were using nakedtime) and are not having increased accidents as a result of doing so.

When you venture out, be prepared. Pack a bag with the following:

- Extra underwear
- A change of clothes (or two!)
- A plastic bag
- A diaper
- Wipes
- A changing mat

And start slow. Choose your first journeys out of the house carefully, limiting them to an hour or so and allowing them to get longer and longer over time. With boys this is all a bit easier, as they can (and love to) pee in the grass. However, the dreaded phrase "I have to poop" is bound to come sooner or later. Hopefully, you are near a bathroom and can get there in time for your little one. If you absolutely can't get to a toilet, I recommend pulling out the diaper and telling your child this is an emergency diaper because there is no toilet available. Otherwise, you risk having a very messy accident on your hands. That is where the plastic bag comes in—should there be an incident, just throw all the clothes in as quick as possible, wipe everything up, and put on the change of clothes.

The Pediatrician

Sometimes there are incidents that necessitate a visit to your child's doctor. As a parent, you have to shoulder a lot of the potty-training burden, but there are some dividing lines that necessitate a call to the pediatrician. How do you know when to call the doc? I have put a few guidelines outlined by the American Academy of Family Physicians[xii] below, but a parent's instinct is the guiding light here. Even if your child's issue doesn't show up on this list, if you feel uneasy about something, call the doctor.

When to call the pediatrician:

- your child isn't daytime potty trained by four years old
- your child isn't nighttime potty trained by five years old
- your child hasn't pooped in three days
- your child pees very little, as in two-three times a day
- your child pees too often, and it comes on suddenly
- it seems like it hurts or is difficult for your child to pee or poop
- there is blood in your child's urine

How Do You Know Your Kid is Potty Trained?

We dedicate a lot of time to talking about knowing if your child is ready to potty train. But how do you know when your child is officially potty trained? Sometimes this happens without us adults even really realizing it.

If you notice that your small potty is gathering dust, your baby uses the bathroom without you, you don't pack spare underwear on outings anymore, and you take car journeys without thinking twice, your baby is potty trained!

If your toddler knows then they need to go, gets there by themselves, and goes to the potty without even bothering to tell you, perhaps informing you when it's all over that they did it, then your baby is potty trained.

Congratulations!

SECTION TEN

~

TOP 10 TIPS FOR POTTY TRAINING, STRAIGHT FROM THE PARENTS WHO'VE BEEN THERE

Sometimes, getting advice from those who have been there recently is the best medicine. There's nothing like having someone give a voice to your worries or sharing a hack that saves you a ton of time. That's why I've saved this section for last—it's the best compilation of tips that I have heard over and over again from parents who have been there. Their tips are all over the board, but they are the most prevalent feedback I get and speak to the truly important aspects of potty training, which is why I've distilled them for you in a single chapter.

1. Maintain The Positive Attitude

"At the day care where I work, I know all the parents and children very well. When it comes time to potty train, we always notice that the parents who generally treat their children like small individuals and have loads of patience are the ones whose children potty train smoothly. The nervous and nagging parents are typically the ones that have more issues and whose children are less cooperative."

-Denise, 28, day-care worker

This is the golden rule of potty training. Think of it more like a party: a time to smile, to celebrate, and to exercise your patience with unwelcome guests, like accidents and tantrums. This positivity will pay dividends!

2. Short & Sweet

"With our second, we were a lot more lenient, since things went so well with the first. We sort of let her lead the way on the toilet, and she would just sit and sit for ages, having fun playing with stuff in the bathroom and just generally not paying attention to the task at hand. We started putting on a timer and limiting her potty time to three minutes, and pretty soon she was 'all business,' in more ways than one!"

-Jenny, 37, mother of three

Don't let your child sit for too long on the potty, or it runs the risk of becoming another place to be and to play rather than the place to do dirty business. Usually, two or three minutes is all the time your child will need, and you can judge pretty easily if they are playing around or not.

3. Hydrate Properly

> *"We were having trouble getting on a potty schedule with my first. It seemed like he just never wanted to go! In the hustle and bustle of that first potty training, I realized I was hardly giving him anything to drink. We upped his liquid intake and suddenly he was going whenever we led him to the potty."*
>
> *- Ursula, 32, mother of two*

Be sure to hydrate properly! Don't overdo it, but make sure your child has six to eight drinks a day. Sodas, caffeine, and sugary drinks don't count and should be avoided.

4. Consistency

> *"I am a single dad, so I have a nanny that helps out while I am at work. My son was taking a long time to potty train, and I found out that she wasn't taking him to the bathroom at scheduled times, instead waiting for him to take the initiative, which he just wasn't ready to do. Once we smoothed out communication so he had a consistent routine, it went so much faster!"*
>
> *-Bryan, 40, father of one*

I can't stress the importance of consistency enough! Your child needs surrounding circumstances to stay constant to be able to learn how to use the potty. Being on the same page as caregivers is so often easy to overlook, but it really is important. Take the time to sit and explain your routine, and write it out and put it somewhere visible.

5. Figure Out Fear and Face It Head On

> *"My first daughter was early to potty train but desperately afraid of doing #2. We didn't understand why, and we tried everything! The doctor told us some kids think that they are flushing away a piece of their body, because of how feces are explained. We bought a book about the process and talked about the digestive system and she immediately started using the toilet to poop."*
>
> *Melanie, 40, mother of four*

Kids can be so literal. That makes for a lot of funny stories, and, of course, some not so funny as well. It's important to get to the bottom of our children's fears when it comes to potty training and, if possible, clear them up in a logical, understandable way. You may find that what is blocking your child is easily fixable.

6. My Best Friend, The Potty

> *"When we started potty training, I thought of the potty as a new friend for my son, and I treated it that way. We introduced him slowly but surely, played up all the potty's fun parts, and in general spoke about it often. I am convinced this smoothed over the training and helped him train in record time!"*
>
> *-Daniel, 35, father of one*

Every little bit helps, and if you knew you could smooth the potty-training road somehow, wouldn't you do it? It can start with changing your child's diapers in the same room as the potty, beginning to trace a connection for your little one. Start flushing her number two's in the potty, with them watching. Things like this help to create a connection in your child's brain and reduce fear.

7. Don't Ask

> *"My child always said no when I asked him if he had to go. I think he just had better things to do! Because he definitely did most of the time, and it led to accidents everywhere. When I stopped asking him if he had to go and told him it was 'Potty Minute,' he immediately started racking up success after success."*
> -Ben, 33, father of one

There is a world of difference in your children's ear between "Tell me when you have to go" and "Do you want to go." What kid ever wants to leave their food, toys, or friends to go to the potty? Think about it, and then stop asking. Just do it.

8. Have More Than One Potty

> *"We weren't having any luck potty training my daughter... she would have accidents all the time, usually on the way to the potty. Our house is kind of big, so I decided to get a few more potties to spread out around the house. It worked! With more options nearby, she potty trained in no time."*
>
> -Jesse, 28, mother of one

Many parents swear by having more than one potty—especially those who live in multi-floor homes. It helps if these potties are exactly alike to reinforce the link between the object and the behavior.

9. Help Them Get Something Out

> *"We would celebrate even just a few drops of pee when my son was first beginning to potty train. He would get super bummed if he couldn't go when we went to the bathroom, so to help him reframe the situation, I insisted that even a drop or two was great! He loved it and soon forgot all about any pressure he had been putting on himself."*
>
> -Janice, 40, mother of three

Potty training is all about tallying up lots of small successes. When you begin, don't worry about the end goal just yet; focus on helping your child celebrate the smallest advances. This positivity will motivate your child to continue advancing until the ultimate goal is reached—100% potty trained!

10. Avoid The Power Struggle

> *"I thought it was time to potty train my daughter, so we started the whole shebang. She wasn't having any of it, and I couldn't tell where the root of this resistance was coming from. I found myself threatening and getting into arguments that had no winner. We decided to take a break, and when we tried again two months later, it was a breeze."*
>
> *-Caroline, 30, mother of one*

A power struggle and fight over the potty is only going to make matters worse and the struggle longer. A situation of total resistance is best left to time. Anything to avoid pitting you against your child as equals in the long term. You will likely find that taking it back up later means your child is much more predisposed to cooperate.

SECTION ELEVEN

~

CONCLUSION

Well, here we are, at the end of this book, full of the best advice I have from my experience, both personal and workplace. If you take only one thing away from this book, I want it to be this: potty training is not a scary, horrible moment in time. It is normal; everyone goes through it, and it is never as big a deal as people make it out to be. As parents, the best thing we can do is see the process through our child's eyes.

Empathy and safety are the two best things you can offer to your child during potty training and beyond. Challenging situations will crop up in you and your child's life from now until eternity, so learning how to process these situations and get through them together is wonderful practice for the road ahead. Your child is taking steps toward independence, and this is something to be celebrated, indeed.

Congratulations to both of you!

YOU CAN CHANGE MY LIFE

I hope this book has given you value. I'm positive that if you follow what I've written, you will be on your way to stress free potty training your child in no time. You can change your child's life through positive potty training.

I have a tiny favor to ask. If you liked the book, would you mind taking a minute to write your feedback on Amazon about it? I check all my reviews and love to get feedback (that's the real reward for the months of work that went into writing this book—knowing that I'm helping people).

Use the link or scan the QR code below to leave a review on Amazon.com

https://amzn.to/2Ztdvh7

SCAN ME

Practical Positive Potty Training

Use the link or scan the QR code below to leave a review on Amazon.co.uk

https://amzn.to/3meW4uw

SCAN ME

Now, I don't just want to sell you a book—I want to see you put the advice outlined in this book into action. As you work toward your goals, however, you'll probably have questions or may run into some difficulties. I'd like to be able to help you with these! I answer questions from readers every day.

Here's how we can connect:

Email: Hannah@AtmosPublishing.com

Keep in mind I get a lot of emails every day, and answer everything personally, so if you can keep yours as brief as possible, it helps me ensure everyone gets helped!

Also, if you have any friends or family who might enjoy this book, spread the love, and lend it to them! Or do better!

Email them and me in the same email and **I'll send them the eBook or paperback version for free!**

Thanks again and I wish you the best!

Hannah

P.S.

If you didn't like the book, please send me an email with your comments. I take all constructive criticism seriously and will do my best to improve the book.

HANNAH'S OTHER BOOKS & NEW RELEASES

Sign up to be the first to know about Hannah's new books and get early copies as well as audiobooks **for free** using the link or QR code below.

https://bit.ly/2FIV4hF

SCAN ME

References

[i] Engelhart, K. (2014, June 23). The Powerful History of Potty Training. Retrieved June 21, 2020, from https://www.theatlantic.com/health/archive/2014/06/the-surprisingly-political-history-of-potty-training/371512/

[ii] Au, S., & Ph.D., S. P. (2015). Stress-Free Potty Training: A Commonsense Guide to Finding the Right Approach for Your Child (Second ed.). New York, NY: AMACOM.

[iii] Crider, C. (2020, April 28). Potty Training Methods: Which Is Right for Your Child? Retrieved June 27, 2020, from https://www.healthline.com/health/childrens-health/potty-training-methods#methods

[iv] The Evolution of Potty Training. (n.d.). Retrieved July 3, 2020, from https://priceonomics.com/the-evolution-of-potty-training/

[v] Dewar, G., PhD. (n.d.). Infant toilet training: The scientific evidence. Retrieved July 3, 2020, from https://www.parentingscience.com/infant-toilet-training.html

[vi] Toilet Training. (n.d.). Retrieved June 7, 2020, from https://www.hopkinsmedicine.org/health/wellness-and-prevention/toilettraining

[vii] Potty training: How to get the job done. (2019, October 5). Retrieved June 28, 2020, from https://www.mayoclinic.org/healthy-lifestyle/infant-and-toddler-health/in-depth/potty-training/art-20045230

[viii] Brucks, B., & Daum, F. (2016). *Potty Training*. Van Duuren Media.

[ix] Pantley, E. (2006). The No-Cry Potty Training Solution: Gentle Ways to Help Your Child Say Good-Bye to Diapers: Gentle Ways to Help Your Child Say Good-Bye to Diapers (Pantley) (1st ed.). McGraw-Hill Education.

[x] Glowacki, J. (2015). Oh Crap! Potty Training: Everything Modern Parents Need to Know to Do It Once and Do It Right (1) (Oh Crap Parenting) (First Paperback Edition). Gallery Books.

[xi] Kapferer, M. (2019, March 27). How to potty train a girl. MadeForMums. https://www.madeformums.com/toddler-and-preschool/how-to-potty-train-a-girl/

Printed in Great Britain
by Amazon